THE OFFICIAL BOOK OF THE INTERNATIONAL OLYMPIC COMMITTEE AND
THE ORGANIZING COMMITTEE OF THE XVI OLYMPIC WINTER GAMES

ALBERTVILLE 92

XVI OLYMPIC WINTER GAMES ALBERTVILLE MCMXCII
SAVOIE-FRANCE 8th-23th FEBRUARY, 1992
B A C K   T O   N A T U R E

ALBERTVILLE OOOOO 92 ®

C O N T E N T S

Over seven years have passed since the day the XVI Olympic Winter Games were entrusted to Albertville/Savoie. Today, as they draw to a close, I can say, as President of the International Olympic Committee, that they have lived up to our highest expectations. Ever since the flame arrived on French soil, France has expressed with tremendous energy an enthusiasm which has fired imaginations all over the world.

On behalf of the entire Olympic and sporting family, I would like to express my most sincere congratulations and all my gratitude to the organizing committee, masterfully led by its Co-Presidents Michel Barnier and Jean-Claude Killy. In the impressive setting of the French Alps, they have controlled constantly and with brio the difficulties inherent to the vast and varied theatre of these XVI Winter Games.

Their judgement has been proved right and our confidence in them deserved. Today, as the Games close, they have earned our praise. Thanks to their tenacity and that of their entire team, superbly backed up by thousands of volunteers, these Games will go down in Olympic history as a true success.

In an atmosphere of friendship and pride, the world's most highly trained athletes, supported by their National Olympic Committees, took the stage one by one, each in his or her speciality, on snow and on ice, to give the best of themselves in venues which, with the help of the International Federations,offered highly testing conditions even for the best. The feats they performed were relayed all over the world with, as always, the very latest advances in broadcasting techniques.

With this book, we are bringing you a day-by-day account of the glorious competitions we have just witnessed. I hope that these fantastic images, never to be forgotten by those who saw them live, will enable every one of you to experience something of the thrill which so frequently charged the atmosphere of these XVI Winter Games.

Juan Antonio Samaranch
IOC President

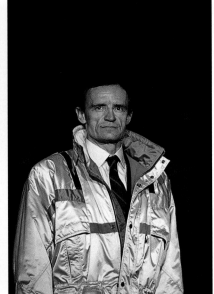

The most beautiful story of the XVI Olympic Winter Games is told in the moments of happiness and shared emotion.
There we remember gestures, glances, objects, colours and light.
The collection of images beautifully assembled in this official book make up the album of our memory.
We will never forget.

Michel Barnier   Jean Claude Killy
Presidents of the Organizing Committee of the XVI Olympic Winter Games of Albertville and Savoie

ALBERTVILLE '92, BACK TO NATURE

The coat of arms of Charles-Albert, the founder of Albertville.

The XVI olympic winter games of Albertville and of Savoie,
were a dream come true for Jean-Claude Killy.
A successful games, for the honour of the people of France.

The XVIth Winter Olympic Games in Albertville, in Savoie, were a dream come true for Jean-Claude Killy. A successful Games, for the honour of the people of France, was an ambition surpassing even those historic three gold medals for skiing which the mountain boy from Val d'Isère had won way back in 1968, at the Games of Grenoble and the last time that France had been Olympic host. The Games in Albertville were the fulfilment of a concept that had taken root in the early Eighties.

Yet the dream was also, on the admission of even the most sanguine Frenchman, a logistical nightmare in its planning by Jean-Claude Killy and Michel Barnier, his co-president of the organizing committee. Embracing 13 different site facilities at a lot of separate mountain towns and villages, spread over thousands of square kilometers of tortuous narrow valleys, it presented a challenge without parallel. «It has been both an advantage and a disadvantage» Jean-Claude Killy said the day before the Opening Ceremony. «We are aware of the problems of communication, but the advantage is the tradition and experience in winter sports events of our well known centres, and the will of the people of Savoie to make the Games memorable.»

The Games had been awarded to Albertville by the International Olympic Committee, at their Session in Lausanne, Switzerland in 1986: in the opinion of many as a compensation for France when preferring Barcelona to Paris as host for the Summer Games in the same year. The emotional, eloquent address by Premier Jacques Chirac at the presentation could not be denied some reward ! Then it remained for J.C. Killy, M. Barnier and their committee to meet the challenge.

A US$ 1.7 billion programme began to modernise the region, with massive improvements to rail and road connections, internally in Savoie and from outside. Huge investments were made in the construction of new sports facilities. Complaints from the ecological lobby, sensitive to the environmental issues of the Vallée Tarentaise, were met by the installation of new water purifiers and rubbish incinerators.

For the region of Savoie, the priorities are no different from much of the rest of the world: to generate employment and prosperity for this 900 year old community of mountain farmers and cheese producers, without further harm to the exquisite and picturesque landscape of forests and mountain passes. In planning to avoid a transport thrombosis, the organizing committee created a communication programme of thousands of cars and buses more complex than that of an invading army, eliminating casual private travel. It was a programme that would need fortune and the weather to smile upon it.

Savoie, a region with a long history.

Relative calm, Albertville at night.

Each town and village, from Albertville with its population of 18,000 to tiny Pralognan where the demonstration sport of curling was to be staged, threw themselves whole-heartedly into the venture, praying that the expected 800,000 visitors and the revenue from television and sponsors would justify the investment.

«We're no longer a sad little city» proclaimed the municipal magazine of Albertville, now boasting a new theatre and handsome arcades shopping plaza. The people of Savoie worked hard at the unaccustomed role of welcoming that vast influx of foreigners from around the world. One of the virtues of sport is its cure for xenophobia.

Given the need for decentralisation, Moûtiers, the medieval town at the conjunction of four valleys, seemed the obvious choice as International Broadcasting Centre.

Up the road at the main Olympic Village in Brides-les-Bains, with its hot springs and newly renovated thermal baths, the athletes enjoyed a mountain intimacy that was a throw-back to Winter Games of past years. For the week preceding the Games, Courchevel, regular destination of the social jet-setters, hummed with the deliberations of the Session and of the IOC's Executive Board, and entranced the more athletic members with the beauty of its ski runs.

Olympic tourists found their way around the expanse of sites with glossy brochures in four languages, and multinational businessmen from the exclusive corporate sponsors, who exchange expertise more easily at the bar or in the restaurant than on the dance floor *après ski*, were doing their bit to help Savoie meet its costs. The grandeur of Savoie's Alps was once again the back-drop to the grandeur of the Winter Games.

The huge ice hall where 9,000 spectators marvelled at the figure skating.

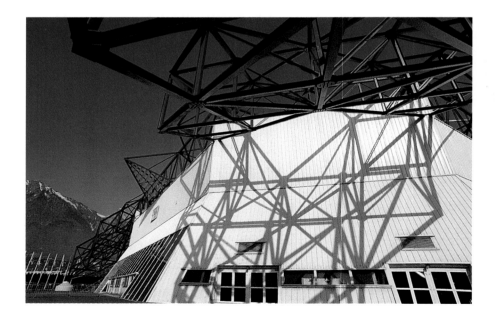

Notre Dame de la Vie, the baroque chapel in St Martin de Belleville, along the road to Les Menuires, the slalom venue.

Les Saisies, cross country host for the Games.

Next page
Albertville's metamorphosis: Le Dome, the brand-new cultural centre in Place de l'Europe, heart of the Olympic Cultural Festival.

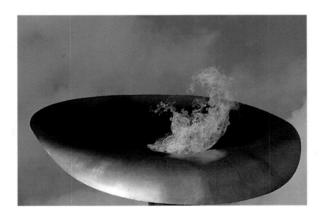

»This is why the flame extinguished here will spring to life there. The wind of the moment will be all it takes to carry the flame around the world.«

Pierre de Coubertin

ETERNAL FLAME

A t 5 p.m. on February 8, the last torchbearer had approached the gigantic bowl on the site of the Opening Ceremony in Albertville to light the flame that will watch over the XVI Olympic Winter Games for fifteen days. This magical gesture, imbued with solemnity and emotion, had ended the fantastic relay organized by the French Post Office. On December 14, the torch had been flown from Olympia to Paris on board Concorde. Before arriving in Albertville, it was carried over 5,000 kilometres by 5,000 young people between 15 and 20 years old escorted by 1,000 post office workers. In all, the Torch had crossed 67 French departments, 57 towns and cities and more than 2,000 villages. A number of events on the theme of light was accompanying it along the way.

December 13th, 1991, the traditional ceremony in ancient Olympia, Greece for the departure of the Flame to the XVI Olympic Winter Games in Albertville.

For the first time in Olympic history, the creation of the Torch has been entrusted to a famous designer, the distinguished Philippe Starck, laureate of several French design awards (Creator of the Year 1985, Knight of Arts and Letters ...), also known as «builder, futurologist, adventurer ...»

Starck chose brushed stainless steel from Ugine for this original stream-lined Torch. It is a supreme representation of the immateriality of things, where the Torch is overshadowed by the Flame.

5,000 youngsters carried the Olympic Torch from Paris through 67 *départements* and 57 towns.

Michel Barnier and Jean-Claude Killy accompanying the Olympic Flame from Athens to Paris on Concorde.

Explosion of colour, youth and joy along the route of the Olympic Flame.

Hand in hand, the athlete Michel Platini with young hopeful François Grange.

Left page
Les Champs Elysées under snow,
a show to rival even the
Bicentenary of the French
Revolution.

DAY

France set a standard for all time in elegance,
artistry and emotion, bringing joy to their own people
and admiration from the rest of the world.

ALL IS MAGICAL, ... MEMORABLE

Ode to lightness and grace.

The President of France, François Mitterrand is met by IOC President Juan Antonio Samaranch.

Seldom if ever has there been such grandeur, that abstract definition of man's nobler moments, as in the Opening Ceremony staged in Albertville's temporary open-air stadium on a star-lit, unforgettable evening. François Mitterrand, president of the Republic, formally set in motion the XVI Winter Games, and France set a standard for all time in elegance, artistry and emotion, bringing joy to their own people and admiration from the rest of the world.

As François-Cyril Grange, an eight-year-old schoolboy from St.Jean de Maurienne, stood hand in hand with Michel Platini, symbol of the spirit of French sport, to ignite the Olympic flame, the pair of them silhouetted on the lip of the stadium against dark snow-clad peaks catching the last faint pink of the sunset, man and nature were in harmony.

The home of Baron Pierre de Coubertin retains in its approach to sport that sense of glory that is so distinctive, in success or failure. The Opening Ceremony now epitomised all that is best in man's fragile ambitions. I have never been as moved on such an occasion, and I have witnessed many, as on this evening of colour and costume, art and acrobatics, music and mime.

With the sky still clear and blue, fighter-jets twice roared over-head leaving a trail of coloured smoke of the Olympic rings. Fireworks accompanied an exposition of European unity, and Juan Antonio Samaranch, president of the International Olympic Committee, walked to the open western end of the stadium to greet M. Mitterrand.

Now the competitors of 64 nations marched past. There were sensitive, special cheers for the new nations emerging out of Europe's former configurations. For Estonia in their steel-blue uniforms, for Croatia and Slovenia, for The Unified Team embracing for this year the republics of the Commonwealth of Independent States; for the lone skier from Swaziland. And finally for the host nation, swaggering in their silver suits.

Michel Barnier and Jean-Claude Killy, co-chairmen of the organizing committee, and Samaranch made their formal welcoming speeches. Killy's apt words — «some 2,200 athletes, some of whom are bearing the flags of newly independent nations represented at the Olympics for the first time ... will lead us into the realm of fantastic feats» — rang out across the freezing night air.

As M. Mitterrand spoke his brief words, Alpine horns and church bells echoed through the valleys. Soldiers raised the Olympic flag, and 30,000 upturned silent faces signified the common aspirations among those brought together by the Games. Totally unheralded, Platini appeared with the flame, ran one lap, then joined little François-Cyril, and the two of them mounted the 80 steps to ignite that flame of hope. Surya Bonaly, adopted orphan of Reunion Island, and all of France's hope for a skating gold medal, took the athlete's oath; and 11-year-old Séverine du Pelloux, a Savoie girl, hauntingly sang from a seven metre high platform the Marseillaise. We weep happiness for France.

Extravaganza of light, sound and fantasy: Vive the Olympic Games!

The sky as backdrop for a sublime aerial ballet.

Then come the *Folies*. Men on monster stilts, dancers, jugglers, ballet skaters. The scene and the music changes: accordionists beat out a rhythm for trampolinists, and for magical acrobats suspended from a huge central mast on sponge ropes. In the darkness we catch our breath.

And on it goes. Drummers in snow-flake silver suspended from cranes on perilous mobiles are spotlighted like ghostly Christmas decorations, while statuesque dancers on revolving platforms pirouette in glacial elegance. Arias fill the air. A thousand flags arrive like snow-fall, huge air-filled ribbons balloon sky-wards. All is magical, memorable. Now is the close of the first day of these Games, honour is high; even if France has suffered a narrow 3-2 defeat against the fancied Canadians in the first match of the ice-hockey tournament.

Right page
Europe is represented for the first time by twelve skaters-stars.

A giant horn of plenty spilling
our childhood dreams out into
the stadium.

Acrobats hanging in the air
underneath the giant umbrella.

DAY

2

What an ovation Piccard received
from the packed crowd, gathered around the sauce pan
and able to see so much of the tortuous run on a
morning of unbroken sunshine

THE FAST MEN FAIL

The Olympic men's downhill race is the most revered, the most prestigious, of the Games, yet few were happy with the outcome on a course that drew controversy before and after. Not even the winner, Patrick Ortlieb of Austria, thought it was a test of true downhillers: a course that, with thirty five per cent more bends than most downhills, put the emphasis on skiers much more than on skis.

Ortlieb had never previously won a downhill, and afterwards he was saying that he would not be hurrying back to race on the run specially designed for the Games by the celebrated Bernhard Russi. «It's just too slow» he said. All the fancied fast men, Heinzer of Switzerland, the favourite and World Cup leader, Wasmeier of Germany, and Kitt of the United States, who had won the World Cup event a few weeks before on the Val d'Isère course, finished sixth, fourth and ninth respectively. One man overjoyed was Franck Piccard, the bronze medallist in Calgary four years before and now silver medallist. Ortlieb, first of the day through the gate, had set the standard for the field, descending the Face de Bellevarde in 1 minute 50.37 seconds. None, it seemed, could surpass him, and Mader of Austria and Wasmeir had the scent of silver and bronze when Piccard attacked the leaders from the twenty third starting position.

Other good men had failed to finish, Stock, the veteran Austrian and winner in 1980, had crashed; Girardelli, four times World Cup champion had run off the course. Another was Accola of Switzerland. Piccard's early interval times were not indicative of what was about to happen, for he was in ninth position. Yet mastering the technique of the course, as he swept across the finishing line he was a mere five hundredths of a second behind Ortlieb. What an ovation he received from the packed crowd, gathered around the saucepan and able to see so much of the tortuous run on a morning of unbroken sunshine. Maybe it was the euphoria of the occasion, but Piccard was quick to praise the course, saying that in his opinion it offered

Franck Piccard, warms up before tackling the downhill specially designed for these Games by Bernhard Russi.

«the future of Alpine skiing». Gliding, and therefore ski-science, is not paramount when racers have to spend so much time on their edges, though Piccard denied that it was a course for Super-G skis. For the Frenchman it was an astonishing return to form, because he had recently stopped competing for a while after finishing a dejected 70th at Garmish. Now, it was difficult to stop him talking! «I made a slight mistake at the Ancolie passage, and that cost me the gold medal» he said afterwards.

Another Austrian who had never won a major title but now did so was Ernst Vettori, taking the ski-jump 90-metre gold medal. The disappointment for the crowd at Courchevel was that Toni Nieminen, the 16-year-old Finn who had dominated the World Cup season, missed the chance to become the youngest male champion in the history of the Olympics when he could take only third place. Yet he showed his early maturity, a sense of the uniqueness of the Games, when he said: «It's like a dream and I still can't believe it.»

Vettori gained 222.8 points from his two jumps to defeat his 17-year-old compatriot Martin Höllwarth, who took the silver on 218.1 points. Vettori had behind him 14 victories on the World Cup circuit, but no medals from two previous Olympics. These were the first Olympics to witness the new V-style jumping used by the majority of competitors. Vettori said that his victory was partly dedicated to Jan Bokloev, the Swedish jumper who initiated the technique. The best jump of the day had been Höllwarth's 90.5 metres

The 3rd medal for Austria, won by Ernst Vettori in the K90 jump, ahead of his compatriot Martin Hollwarth and Toni Nieminen of Finland.

A.J. Kitt, United States, won the downhill in Val d'Isère a few weeks ago, but this time placed ninth.

in the first series, but he had a poor second jump. So did Nieminen, who lay second after the first series with his leap of 88 metres.

Evidence that amalgamation has not reduced the effectiveness of the former German Democratic Republic team came with the first and second place in the women's 3,000-metres speed skating event at Albertville Olympic Oval. Gunda Niemann, the world record holder, and Heike Warnicke were comfortably ahead of Emese Hunyady of Austria, who took the bronze.

Grim determination on the face of Dutch skater Lia Van Schie, 9th in the 3,000m speed skating, which was won by the German Niemann.

Applause for Lothar Munder, Brazil, who was 41st

No luck for Christophe Fivel, France, during practice of downhill.

Page 58:
The most important thing is to take part, not necessarily to win! Three cheers for Lamine Gueye from Senegal, who came last in the downhill.

Page 59:
The Austrian Patrick Ortlieb: a golden run in 1:50.37!

DAY

3

«I skied the perfect race, absolutely perfect»
a delighted Ulvang said. «What a day for Norway».
It was a triumph that puts into
better perspective that IOC's awarding to Lillehammer
of Norway the hosting of the 1994 Winter Games
— the Games that change the cycle
of Summer and Winter — an award more than justified
by Norway's position,
prior to Albertville, as joint all-time leaders of Nordic
event medals with the former USSR.

Norway Sweep The Field

Not since Ivar Formo had won the 50 kilometres at Innsbruck - Seefeld in 1976 had Norway won an Olympic race in their national sport of Nordic skiing. Now, at Les Saisies, they triumphantly swept the field in the men's 30 K. Such was the celebrating that none had time to reflect too much on a less propitious event, their 8-1 drubbing by l'Equipe Unifiée — the Russians — in the ice-hockey first round at Méribel.

Vegard Ulvang, 28, had been a bronze medalist in Calgary and also in last year's World Championship. He came to the race as current World Cup leader, and the sternest of battles developed with his compatriot Bjorn Daehlie. At the half way stage, Daehlie was leading, but Ulvang, on a high-altitude course ranging between 1,500 and 2,000 metres that demands the ultimate in aerobic fitness, overhauled his colleague to win in 1 hr. 22 mins 27.8 secs, some 46 seconds ahead of Daehlie. Terje Langli was another half a minute behind in third place.

»I skied the perfect race, absolutely perfect» a delighted Ulvang said. «What a day for Norway!». It was a triumph that puts into better perspective IOC's awarding to Lillehammer of Norway the hosting of the 1994 Winter Games — the Games that change the cycle of Summer and the Winter — an award more than justified by Norway's position, prior to Albertville, as joint all-time leaders of Nordic event medals with the former USSR.

Indeed, the Norwegians had another skier in fifth place, Erling Jevne, just behind Marco Albarello of Italy. The cries of «Heia Norge» rang loud and long in the pine-scented air, on the best day this country has known. The Norwegians are true fanatics at their sport. Ulveng's idea of a holiday last year was a trip to Mt. McKinley in Alaska, followed by a 600 km trek across Greenland.

There was no holding Bonnie Blair of the United States in the women's 500 metres speed skating at Albertville. Blair, of Champaign, Illinois, retained her Calgary title, though more than a second outside her Olympic record with a time of 40.33 seconds. This still gave her eighteen hundredths to spare over Ye Qiaobo of China, with Christa Luding of Germany, champion and runner-up in the past two Olympics, now taking the bronze. The race had to be postponed half an hour because warm temperatures, in the continuous sunshine at the outdoor Oval, caused moisture to gather.

Ye's silver medal was China's first in any Winter Olympics. She skated three pairs before Blair, setting the American a target that was fast but within her compass. Blair, 27, was supported noisily from the ring-side by brothers, sisters, cousins and her mother and her boyfriend. Qiaobo, prominent for several years, failed a drug test prior to the Games in Calgary, and was suspended for 15 months. The banned substance is, apparently, commonplace in publicly available Chinese medicine. Skating in the second pair with Elena Tiouchiakova (EUN), Qiaobo was impeded on a cross-over when Tiouchiakova failed to give way on the inside; a momentary enforced pause could have been sufficient to cost Qiaobo the gold.

At La Plagne, the men's single luge was won by Georg Hackl of Germany, the runner up in Calgary. Twice world champion, Hackl set a formidable standard, with the fastest time in three of the four runs, including both on the second

At Tignes, Fabrice Becker of France earns a gold medal for his freestyle demonstration. Switzerland's Conny Kissling once again dominates in the women's final.

American fans were not disappointed by Bonnie Blair - who could doubtless skate before she could walk!

day, and having established a course record in his first run on the first day. Markus Prock and Markus Schmidt, both Austrians, were second and third, with the defending Olympic champion, Jens Muller of Germany, finishing fifth, behind Norbert Huber of Italy.

The major surprise of the day was the second successive failure by Marc Girardelli. Having skied off the course in the Downhill, he now fell in the Combined event downhill to see his hopes of any medal evaporate.

Germany's Markus Wasmeier, 4th in the Olympic downhill at Val d'Isère, places 7th in the downhill of the combined, and ends up in 5th place

Left page:
V. Ulvang, seen here in action, B. Daehlie and T. Langli earn three medals for Norway.

DAY

4

This day saw some firsts at Les Saisies.
In the inaugural biathlon for women, Anfissa Reztsova
of the Unified Team won her first medal since converting
to the discipline from skiing.

STROLZ ERROR DECISIVE

After four days of the Games, Alpine skiing was still waiting for the sensational story. For the moment, it continued to get upsets. If the result of the Men's Downhill had been a surprise, so too was the Combined. Josef Polig and Gianfranco Martin of Italy, winners of the gold and silver, were as unheralded as had been Ortlieb, and it is no more than the truth to say that they owed their success to the misfortune, or misjudgement, of other men. The Olympics, no less than life, is about luck as well as ability.

With Girardelli and Mader already out of contention after the downhill section of the Combined, the front end of the field was further thinned by the disasters befalling Hubert Strolz, the Austrian winner of the gold medal in Calgary, and the current Swiss favourite, Paul Accola. Like Ortlieb, Polig and Martin had reason to be modest about their success. Polig admitted that he had not skied well, that he had been lucky.

The result turned on Strolz's bizarre mistiming when only three gates from the finishing line. Accelerating when he should have played it safe, he missed a gate and the medal was gone. This was a more devastating reverse than that of Accola, who was well placed after a sound downhill performance, which had left him lying third. Now, on the first of the two slalom runs, he misjudged a park near the top and was left with a time-margin impossible to close.

If the success of the Italians was low-key, the behaviour afterwards of the French and Swiss federations was considered by many to be low-class. They protested that advertisements carried on the Italians' uniforms had exceeded the 50 square centimetre limit. «It is only by the smallest fraction, and the protest seems less than sporting» observed Gianfranco Kasper, general secretary of the International federation. The federation was to review the situation: Polig and Martin received their medals. The bronze went a Swiss, Steve Locher, whose second place on the two slalom runs gave him the edge over Jean-Luc Cretier of France.

This day saw some firsts at Les Saisies. In the inaugural biathlon for women, Anfissa Reztsova of the United Team won her first medal since converting to the discipline from skiing. At Calgary, Reztsova had won silver in the 20K race and gold in the 4 x 5K relay. Following marriage and the birth of a daughter, she found her husband being a coach in biathlon. Erratic marksmanship is compensated by excellence on skis; although she missed the shooting target three times, she overcame the three "penalty" loops that a racer must then include, to force Antje Miserskay of Germany into second place, with Reztsova's compatriot Elena Belova taking the bronze.

The course could not have been more demanding for women's first entry to the Olympics, with its altitude of over 5,000 feet. There has been international women's biathlon for the past eight years, and their Olympic inclusion for 1992 was agreed at Calgary.

In ice-hockey, the United States, hoping to erase memories of its seventh place in Calgary and its poor defense, gave a sound display in defeating Germany 2-0 at Méribel, thanks to fine work by goal-tender Leblanc, who kept out more than 40 shots. In Calgary the U.S. team had conceded 31 goals in six games. The U.S. had won their opening match here against Italy 6-3 after being 2-3 down.

A first in Les Saisies: women competing for the biathlon title.

Forza Italia: medals for Polig and Martin.

Next page:
Three Austrians ahead in the standings after the first two runs in women's single luge.

Canada celebrates as Isabelle
Brasseur and Lloyd Eisler mount
the podium.

60.
Natalia and Arthur win favour
with the judges - nine 5.9s for
artistic impression - and with
the public.

Next page:
Guy of France and the Austrian
Sulzenbacher battle for victory
in the Nordic Combined.

DAY

There were more than 200 villagers
from Mouthe, half the population of Guy's home,
to cheer his attempt at Courchevel. Even the village
priest was there, the whole group
having left at 3.00 in the morning. There was an air of
euphoria long before the finish.
Their man was to win by a margin wide
enough for time to have drunk a beer before his
compatriot crossed the line.

FRENCH TRIUMPH

The Games had been needing a French triumph. There was Piccard's silver in the Downhill, yet every host nation longs to be acclaimed as much for its own sporting skill as for its hospitality. Predictable but none the less welcome was the victory in Nordic Combined by Fabrice Guy. To make the occasion even sweeter, Silvain Guillaume accompanied him with the silver medal, three points ahead of Klaus Sulzenbacher of Austria.

Guy's victory was never in doubt, achieved with the same decisive style as in the World Cup. In the early stages of the 15 kilometres there was little to chose between Guy

Page 78
1,500m speedskating: Seiko Hashimoto of Japan in third position behind the two Germans Boerner and Niemann.

Two Germans on the 10km biathlon sprint podium: Mark Kirchner, triple world champion the previous year in Lahti, and Ricco Gross.

and the two Austrians, Sulzenbacher and Klaus Ofner, who was eventually to finish fifth. It is Guy's practice to begin to apply the pressure only after five kilometres or so. And so it was now.

There were more than 200 villagers from Mouthe, half the population of Guy's home, to cheer his attempt at Courchevel. Even the village priest was there, the whole group having left at 3.00 in the morning. There was an air of euphoria long before the finish. Their man was to win by a margin wide enough for time to have drunk a beer before his compatriot crossed the line.

There was something special about the medal ceremonies staged by Courchevel in the evening: lines of torch-bearing ski-instructors descending through trees to the podium, fireworks exploding in the crisp night air, a warmth between the local people and the winners. Never was this more so than when Guy and Guillaume ascended the rostrum: Part of the French fairy tale was that Mouthe and Francines-le-Haut, the home of Guillaume, are villages in Jura, in eastern France, no more than ten kilometres apart.

The first double medal winner of the Games was Gunda Niemann of Germany, silver medallist in the women's 1,500 metres speed skating. She had previously taken the gold in the opening event, the 3,000m on Sunday. Now she was the only one to get close to the 2mins 5.87secs winning time of Jacqueline Börner, also of Germany. Seiko Hashimoto was the first to win a medal for Japan in this event, in third place. Uneven ice and a cold wind made conditions difficult; Bonnie Blair, American winner of the 500m, could finish only 21st out of 32 skaters.

Germany and Austria moved to the head of the medal table, thanks in part to respective first and second places in the men's 10K biathlon and the women's single luge. Mark Kirchner and Ricco Gross were well clear, at Les Saisies, of Harri Eloranta of Finland, who was hard pressed for the bronze by Sergei Tchepikov of the Unified Team. Kirchner, an army sergeant from former East Germany, shot two clear rounds and was unchallenged. Germany had all four team members in the first nine.

Doris Neuner and her sister Angelika won Austria's first gold and silver medals in the single luge. Austria's last medal was Helene Thurner's bronze in 1964, the first year of the sport in the Olympic programme. The gap between the sisters was .073secs over four amalgamated runs, Angelika being two years the elder at 22. Susi Erdmann of Germany took the bronze.

Petra Kronberger of Austria, with a potential for winning five Alpine events, placed herself in a commanding

Two medals for Gunda Niemann of Germany: gold in the 3,000m and silver in the 1,500m.

position for the Combined when she had the fastest time in the downhill on the first day, leading Krista Schmidinger by half a second. Kronberger's compatriot, Sabine Ginther, favourite for the Combined, had fallen in practice the previous day and retired home. The course proved confusing for a number of the racers, including American Wendy Fisher, who broke a thumb on the practice run.

Florence Masnada, in a good position for another French medal in the Combined.

Fabrice Guy takes a well-deserved gold in the Nordic Combined, followed by Sylvan Guillaume.

The French team beats the Swiss
4-3 in Méribel.

Next page:
The Incredible crash of Kristine
Krone, U.S.A.

DAY

*Moguls is the most natural, the least
contrived of the three freestyle disciplines. Aerials and
ballet are entertainment, but are they sport
in the true sense? Moguls relate to regular mountain
skiing; and if the blaring rock music that accompanies
the racers down the slope might make de Coubertin want
to turn a deaf ear in his grave, I fancy that the
pragmatic French founder of the Games would welcome
this youthful event so full of joie de vivre.*

MOGULS' JOIE DE VIVRE

Freestyle skiing came of age in a snowstorm at Tignes, in front of a crowd estimated by some at over 10,000. It was another memorable day for the French, who took first, second, fourth and ninth places in the men's final of the Moguls discipline. Raphaelle Monod of France leading the women's qualifiers from the previous day and therefore last down the 250 meter slope, lost control near the finish and was eighth and last.

Moguls is the most natural, the least contrived of the three freestyle disciplines. Aerials and ballet are entertainment, but are they sport in the true sense? Moguls relate to regular mountain skiing; and if the blaring rock music that accompanies the racers down the slope might make de Coubertin want to turn a deaf ear in his grave, I fancy that the pragmatic French founder of the Games would welcome this youthful event so full of joie de vivre. «Freestyle *is* the world» said Nelson Carmichael, the American bronze medallist.

Stine Hattestad of Norway, third in the women's event, agreed with the public perception that Moguls is the closer to real skiing. «We use long skis, and therefore it's more similar» she said, «but you can never do well in ballet or aerials if you can't ski well.» The virtue of freestyle is that the public can see and enjoy the whole of every run, can see and measure the quality of the two compulsory jumps, can agree and disagree with the points awarded on style by the judges. The weakness is that here is another event dependent on arbitrary judgement, for only a quarter of the points are determined by the time.

Spectacular jumps by Carmichael, for the highest points so far - also a quarter of the available total — put him in the lead with Jean-Luc Brassard, a fancied Canadian, and two Frenchmen to come. Brassard was below his best and was seventh. Now came Olivier Allamand, slower than Carmichael but with superb turning - half the available marks -- to take the lead. It was not enough. Edgar Grospiron, last man down, combined the fastest time — how he did not fall was astonishing — with high marks on turns and jumps. The performance was the more remarkable because of rapidly declining visibility. None could challenge the judges' marks on the performance of the world champion. Donna Weinbrecht of America, likewise world champion, only fractionally overhauled the fragile looking Elizaveta Kojevnikova from Moscow to take the lead on the penultimate run. Could Monod surpass her? The answer, sadly for France, was no.

Petra Kronberger, leader from the downhill section of the women's Combined event, came third in the slalom to take the gold medal, and help place Austria at the head of the medal table. The defending champion, Anita Wachter of Austria, was faster than Kronberger over the two slalom runs, but by a margin insufficient to close the gap from the downhill.

Florence Masnada of France took the bronze, ahead of Chantal Bournissen of Switzerland, the country for whom the Games were providing nothing but gloom. After six days, Switzerland had gained no more than a single bronze to lie equal tenth. Krista Schmidinger of America, second in the downhill, fell away with 14th place in the slalom for overall 11th.

Vegard Ulvang of Norway, winner of the 30k Nordic race on the third day, became the first double gold medallist of the Games by winning the 10k event, even though falling midway through the race and breaking a ski pole. A watching friend swiftly handed him a replacement, Although the pole was shorter, Ulvang finished powerfully to be almost half a minute ahead of Marco Albarello of Italy, who also suffered a fall and lost his goggles. Christer Majback of Sweden was third.

Robert Kerstajn of Slovenia in action in the 10km cross-country.

Norway celebrates another win by Ulvang in tough weather conditions.

The snow does not discourage
Wu Jinto of China.

Next page
A new Olympic discipline :
moguls. Edgar Grospiron of
Savoie takes the gold.

Page 94-95
Thirty six athletes battle it out
on the ice in Albertville for the
men' 5,000m speedskating title.

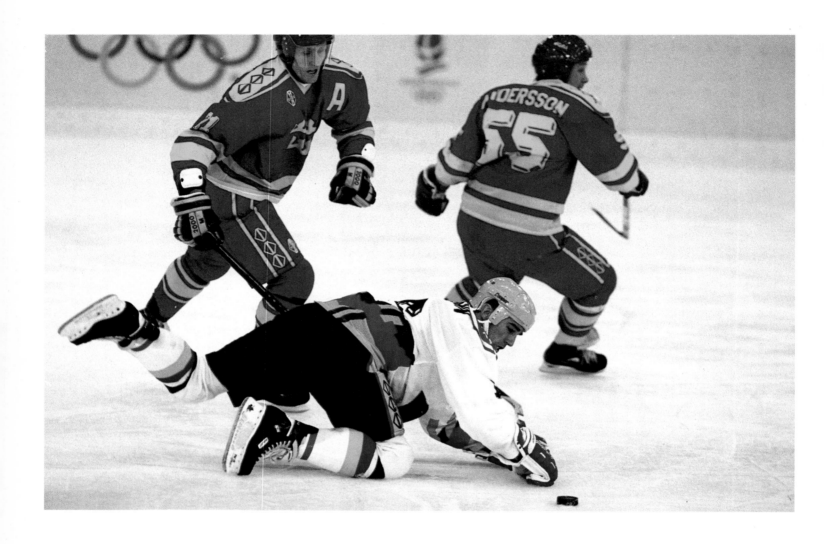

In the qualifiers in Méribel, the Swedish team beat the Germans 3-1.

In Méribel, Petra Kronberger of Austria has a well-deserved win in the women's combined.

DAY

7

*There had been no more dramatic
nor historic a victory throughout the first week. With his
final leap in the 120-metre team ski jump, Toni
Nieminen became the youngest male gold medal winner
ever in the Winter Games.*

BOY-HERO'S SUPREME JUMP

There had been no more dramatic nor historic a victory throughout the first week. With his final leap in the 120-metre team ski jump, Toni Nieminen became the youngest male gold medal winner ever in the Winter Games. His supreme jump of 122 metres snatched victory that had looked a certainty for the confidant Austrians, who had led the competition after the first round.

Under the direction of Toni Innauer, winner of the small hill in 1980 at Lake Placid and now national coach, Austria had hoped for a clean sweep of jumping events at the Albertville Games. Ernst Vettori had taken the opening 90-metre individual event, and now, with Heinz Kuttin, Martin Höllwarth and Andreas Felder, Austria held a psychological edge.

The initial first round had to be terminated, with Vettori, for instance, clearing 125.5 metres, beyond the danger limit. The take-off run was shortened to reduce speed: every kilometre-per-hour at around 95kph is considered to be worth some 10 metres on a jump.

With Höllwarth and Nieminen reaching 123.5 and 123 respectively on the completed first round, the slope was again shortened. The second jump of Nieminen's colleagues — Ari Nikkola, Mikka Laitinen and Risto Laakkonen — was cut by up to eight metres; that of Kuttin, Vettori and Höllwarth by two, three and six metres respectively.

In his glistening, friction-free pink suit, Nieminen swooped down the slope for the last time. Up he soared, spread bat-like in an arc between his skis. As he landed at 122 metres, hundreds of Finnish supporters leaped in joy and disbelief. Felder, needing only 111 metres for victory, was so shocked that he could reach no better than 109.5.

It had been an astonishing turn-around for Finland: after the final jump by Jiri Parma of Czechoslovakia of 115.5, and before Nieminen's leap, Finland had been pushed into third place. The boy-superstar has emerged as worthy successor to the great Matti Nykanen, who won a unique three gold medals in Calgary, including the inaugural team event.

The V-style system, which Austria helped to force the international federation to accept as legal in 1991, and which inflicts a huge G-force on the jumper during the drop, has come naturally to the teenager from Lahti. «He knows no fear» one of his colleagues said afterwards. At the medal ceremony later in the evening, staged at Courchevel-`1850 in an ambience distinctively French and uniquely Alpine, Nieminen spontaneously smiled the smile of a boy. He could have been ten.

Bonnie Blair after winning the 1,000m ahead of Qiaobo Ye and Garbrecht of Germany.

Toni Nieminen jumping for the finish and the gold.

It was another day for the French themselves to bask in satisfaction; Corinne Niogret, Veronique Claudel and Anne Briand won the inaugural women's biathlon relay at Les Saisies. Briand, a veterinary student, was the heroine, regaining the lead on the final leg of 7.5k, and collapsing in an exhausted heap at the finish. Niogret had led the first leg in what was to develop into a three-team battle with Germany and the Unified team. Claudel was overtaken by both teams on the second stage, and it looked a formidable task for Briand when she took over, faced by the World Cup leader Petra Schaaf of Germany.

The drama of the race was intensified by the teams having started together, so that the first across the line was the winner. The final leg by Briand, who could not afford a shooting fault yet had to close the gap along the snow terrain, was an emotional epic in French sport.

At the Albertville Oval, Bonnie Blair of the USA, having become the first to retain the 500 metres title, completed the double in the 1,000 metres. Again Ye Qiaobo of China was second, by the agonisingly close margin of .02 secs.

The French team on top of the
Olympic podium for the
women's 3 x 7.5km biathlon.

Germans take gold and silver in the two-man luge in La Plagne. On the photo, Yves Mankel and Thomas Rudolph, 2nd.

Next page
The Austrians flying above a 23,000-strong crowd at Courchevel.

DAY

Petrenko, with those Slavic eyes and
expressive arms, skated fourth last. There was a
fawn-like grace about his movements, yet his jumps
and spins had a breathtaking athleticism.
He had one fall, and for an awful moment we
supposed that his chance might be in ruins.
The recovery was instant, and when a string of
5,8s for technique and 5,9s for interpretation
flashed up on the scoreboard, we knew he must be
the champion, even though Wylie and Barna
were still to come.

SURPRISE AT MÉRIBEL

For the first time since the evening of the Opening Ceremony, Albertville seemed crowded. The finals of the men's and women's figure skating are always among the most compulsive viewing of the Winter Games, and now the small indoor stadium, barely a quarter the size of the Saddledome in Calgary, could not contain all those wishing to witness the rivalries of the Russians, Americans, Canadians, Czechoslovaks and the rest.

Boitano versus Orser, and Witt versus Thomas, had been two of the highlights of 1988, and now there was a fascinating variety of style in the final group of six men skaters. The favourite was clear: Viktor Petrenko from Ukraine, the bronze medalist in Calgary and runner-up in the world championships of the following two years, was the leader after the original programme. Could he resist the challenge of Kurt Browning of Canada, Petr Barna, the Czech who had taken Petrenko's European title and the effervescent Paul Wylie of America ?

There is something special, in my opinion, about the majority of skaters of the former USSR, now the Unified Team. They have a fluidity, a common balletic feel for the sport, which eliminates much of the apparent contact between skates and ice. This quality was there to be seen now in all three EUN competitors: Viatcheslav Zagorodniuk, Alexei Ourmanov and Petrenko. Zagorodniuk was athletically beautiful. Without any affectation of dress, wearing a simple shirt, he came out like an animal and just skated without inhibition.

Ourmanov, first on the ice of the final group, had a style that was of a single fluid piece, and had that customary choreography that distinguishes the Russians. Browning, by comparison was less technically accomplished than Petrenko, but was equally reminiscent, in his concentric turns, arched backwards, of John Curry, the champion of 1976.

Petrenko, with those Slavic eyes and expressive arms, skated fourth last. There was a fawn-like grace about his movements, yet his jumps and spins had a breathtaking athleticism. He had one fall, and for an awful moment we supposed that his chance might be in ruins. The recovery was instant, and when a string of 5,8s for technique and 5,9s for interpretation flashed up on the scoreboard, we knew he must be the champion, even though Wylie and Barna were still to come.

Wylie, whose sporting career is kept in perspective by his studies at Harvard College, has a relaxed approach that shines out of his smiling eyes. There was a perfect blend between his movement and the music, and an exhilarating confidence in his jumps, the performance receiving a stamping ovation from the crowd. Cat-calls greeted one or two low marks, and three 5,8s and three 5,9s were not enough to bring him better than silver. To my mind, Barna, though technically sound, was somewhat prosaic and unimaginative in taking the bronze.

The women's Downhill, like the men's, produced a totally unexpected result on the Roc de Fer at Méribel. Neither Karrin Lee-Gartner, the winner, from Canada, nor American Hilary Lindh, who took the silver medal, had ever previously won a downhill. Lee-Gartner, who had finished 15th in Calgary — where she lives — had never been higher than third.

»In 1988, my Olympic dream was just a dream», Lee-Gartner said, «but this time I knew it could become a reality. It was the happiest day since my wedding day» (She had married Max Gartner, the former Austrian coach). «Today I felt so strong mentally.»

Lindh, 22, had made an impressive start in the World Cup as a 16-year-old, but failed to progress. «This has been a release for me after six frustrating years» she said. Both skiers, and Veronika Wallinger of Austria in third place, were helped by the fall close to the finish of the fancied Swiss, Chantal Bournissen; and by the fact that Lee-Gartner, starting 12th, had the benefit of better visibility down the course than early starters.

The Canadian Kerrin Lee-
Gartner seized her chance in
Méribel on the Roc de fer.

Gold medal for Viktor Petrenko in men's figure skating; here David Liu of the Chinese Taipei team.

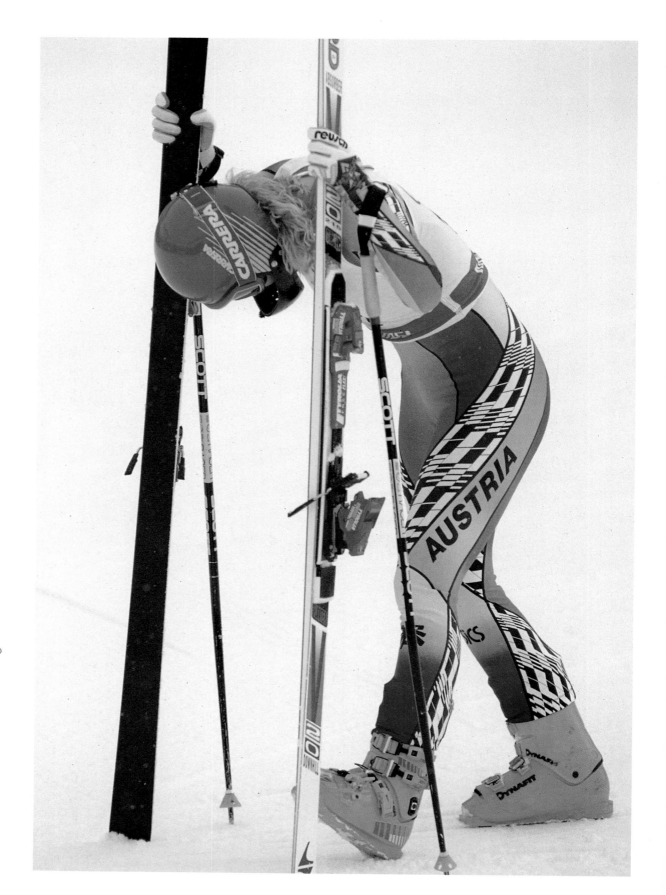

Veronika Wallinger glides to the podium in 1"52"64.

Brian Shimer and Herschel Walker, USA 1, at the start in La Plagne.

Next page:
Two-man bob. Swiss 1 fifth in the standings after two runs.

DAY

9

*The second Sunday of the Games
in Albertville was the most spectacular day so far. The
Swiss won their first gold medal in a volatile two-man
bobsleigh event; young Toni Niemenen became
the star of 1992 — unless Alberto Tomba could emulate
him — with his dominance of the Ski jump; the
rampaging Norwegians, lying fourth in the medal table,
took first and third in the men's Super-giant slalom; the
Germans became the first non-Soviet team to win the
men's biathlon relay since it entered the programme in
1968; and, for the first time, France qualified for the
medal round — or quarter-final round
as it now is — of ice-hockey.*

SWISS BOB'S FACE-SAVER

Page 116
Marie Lindgren of Sweden takes silver in the aerials, behind Colette Brand of Switzerland.

Marc Girardelli wins, at last, a medal in the Super-G in Val d'Isère.

The second Sunday of the Games in Albertville was the most spectacular day so far. The Swiss won their first gold medal in a volatile two-man bobsleigh event; young Toni Niemenen became the star of 1992 — unless Alberto Tomba could emulate him — with his dominance of the Ski jump; the rampaging Norwegians, lying fourth in the medal table, took first and third in the men's Super-giant slalom; the Germans became the first non-Soviet team to win the men's biathlon relay since it entered the programme in 1968; and, for the first time, France qualified for the medal round — or quarter-final round as it now is — of ice-hockey.

There was drama on the controversially expensive and ecologically intrusive bob-run at La Plagne, where swirling low cloud delayed the start of the second day's third and fourth runs. Britain-1, driven by Mark Tout, had led the first day, thanks to the fastest time on either day in the first run; but by the end they slipped back to sixth, partially disconcerted by a long delay at the start of their third run because of failure in the timing mechanism.

Current form now asserted itself. Gustav Weder, a physical education teacher from Zurich, had recently won the European two-man championships at Koenigsee. Although ninth on the first run, he and Donat Acklin had finished the first day lying fifth, and moved into the overall lead by one hundredth of a second with the fastest third run, ahead of Italy-1, driven by Gunther Huber.

The final run could not have been more tense. Weder retained first place again with the fastest time, but, with an identical time, Rudolph Lochner and Markus Zimmerman in the German first bob jumped from fifth place to take the silver medal. German exultation mounted when Christoph Langen and Gunther Eger, their second crew, recorded the third fastest final run to overhaul both Italy-1 and Austria-2 for the bronze medal. It was a face-saver for the Swiss by Weder.

Norway's forte is, traditionally, the Nordic events, but now Kjetil Aamodt and Jan Einar Thorsen gave their country a different gloss by winning the gold and bronze respectively in the Super-G Alpine event; yet another surprise result in this «senior» winter sport. Although Aamodt was runner-up in the world championship last season, he is regarded as a specialist in slalom. He revealed his competitive steel, for earlier this year he had been unwell, and on the morning of the race the schedule was twice altered because of changing weather, the course also being shortened by 150 metres.

It would even have been a clean sweep of the medals for Norway, but for Marc Girardelli of Luxembourg regaining his touch. Following falls in Downhill and Combined, he snatched the silver. It was an unhappy morning for Franck Piccard, the defending champion and second in the Downhill. He fell near the top of the course on an easy section. Aamodt and Girardelli, third and fourth out of the gate, had the advantage of being early on the soft fresh snow. By the time Piccard started, at No. 15, the course was deeply rutted.

Toni Nieminen's performance in the 120-metre ski jump was, without exaggeration, sensational. Having already won the team event for Finland at the last gasp, he now again outclassed the field with two massive leaps of 122 and then 123 metres. The 16-year-old Finn said afterwards that his success in the team event had given him the confidence to be relaxed in the individual jump. And how it showed! Austrians took second and third places: the 17-year-old Martin Höllwarth the silver with jumps of 120.5 and 116.5, and Heinz Kuttin the bronze.

Triumph for the Germans in men's 4x7.5km. In the photo, Geir Einang of the Norwegian team, which finished fifth.

There was euphoria at the Méribel ice-hockey stadium as France beat Norway 4-2, with two goals each from Patrick Dunn and Philippe Bozon. France thereby finished fourth in its group, and would now meet the top team from the other group, dependent on the result between the U.S., so far unbeaten, and Sweden.

Norwegian epic in Val d'Isère: Aamodt, seen in the photo, Torsen, on the podium and Furuseth, 4th.

Page 121
Finals of the freestyle skiing aerials, a demonstration sport: silver in Calgary, bronze in Albertville for Didier Meda.

Pages 122-123
Maia Usova and Alexander Zhulin (EUN) in the original dance.

Klimova and Ponomarenko give of their best to the music of Shostakovich.

Mark Tout and Lenox Paul of Britain in La Plagne.

DAY

*Within half a minute of Klimova and
Ponomarenko being on the ice, we knew the result.
Their style was irreproachable and there was between
them a special kind of unity:
Marina with that soulful, anguished expression
of Cher, the singer, Sergei with a controlled yet strident
masculinity. For four minutes they kept us riveted.*

RUSSIANS' FLOWING SYMMETRY

Page 126
The children of Savoie presented the loveliest flowers and smiles to the athletes. All the costumes were designed by Philippe Guillotel.

In difficult conditions, the Unified Team won the gold medal in the 4x5km relay ahead of Norway and Italy.

The Canadians cannot manage to shake Russian domination.

I t was, in the end, the difference between Bernstein and Bach. Isabelle and Paul Duchesnay had us bewitched with their interpretation of *West Side Story*, but Marina Klimova and Sergei Ponomarenko had that classic poise with which there could be no argument. The climax of the Ice-Dance programme was the predicted and long-awaited duel, the clash of the former Canadians representing France and the Ukrainian and the Russian representing the Unified Team. The Russian married couple gave us that combination that lived up to their own publicity writer. Lofty and earthly.

There was an inspirational quality about Klimova and Ponomarenko, brought to their flowing symmetry. Both they and Maia Usova and Alexander Zhulin, who took the bronze, had that synchronisation of feet, that touch of Rogers and Astaire, for which the judges look, rather than for show-business novelty. There is a fine line between fun and technical refinement. The Italian couple, Stefania Calegari and Pasquale Camerlengo, who came fifth, gave us fun: a blend of Moulin Rouge and New Orleans that pleased the crowd more than the judges.

Yet we should not be patronising about Ice-Dance and the narrow distinction between sport and entertainment. Dance has not the jumps of pairs figure-skating, but more scope for interpretation. What is more, there is no stimulant in this sport other than that of the search for excellence.

Now, the French and Russian couples gave us distinction. Yet if the Duchesnays sent a tingle of excitement running down the spine, Isabelle with her dazzling lifts of *him*, there was no escaping the quality of winners. Following the compulsory and original sections, the Duchesnays were second to Klimova and Ponomarenko, whose world title they took last year. Yet to win, the Duchesnays had to finish *two* places ahead of them on the free programme: a near impossibility.

Within half a minute of Klimova and Ponomarenko being on the ice, we knew the result. Their style was irreproachable and there was between them a special kind of unity: Marina with that soulful, anguished expression of Cher, the singer, Sergei with a controlled yet strident masculinity. For four minutes they kept us riveted. Brother and sister could not generate the same level of passion, yet still gave a consummate display for their devout audience, who could go home content that honour had been saved.

The Olympic Games are for the youth of the world. Miruts Yifter of Ethiopia proved an exception when he achieved the long-distance track double in 1980, at the reputed age of 36. Now, Raisa Smetanina of the Unified Team surpassed that. Twelve days before her fortieth birthday, skiing the second lap of the women's 20-kilometre relay, she earned her tenth Olympic medal, and her fourth gold. Over a span of 16 years, commencing at Insbruck in 1976, she also has five silvers and a bronze.

The women's 5,000m speedskating ended with a German triple. Niemann, twice world champion, Warnicke and Pechstein

Smetanina had been a Soviet champion at Nordic events twenty one times, and seven times a world champion, and had been talking of retirement ever since 1980. She previously shared the record of nine medals with Sixten Jernberg, the Swedish cross-country skier, who competed from 1956 to 1960. Smetanina began her 5k leg with a lead, but had relinquished it by the change-over. «I realised I couldn't do as well as I hoped,» she said, «but I'm happy because it may be my last gold medal.»

Gunda Niemann, Heike Warnicke and Claudia Pechstein made it a clean sweep for Germany in the women's 5,000 metres speed skating. Niemann, who had already won the 3,000 event and come second in the 1,500, was fighting off a bout of influenza, in spite of which she won by a margin of 7 seconds. A number of skaters had been struck down by "flu, including the 1988 triple gold medallist Yvonne van Gennip, would-be defender of the 5,000 title.

The USA and Sweden finish
3-3 in front of 6,100 spectators.

Facing page:
Ray Leblanc, scorer for the
American team.

Next page:
Maia Usova and Alexander
Zhulin begin their dance to the
music of Vivaldi's «Four Seasons».

The German team beats the
Japanese 9-7 in curling.

The Duchesnays' last amateur performance brings them silver.

DAY

*Maybe it was simply the adrenalin
that the Olympic Games generate in a great competitor.
At the first interval-time on the second run Tomba was
twelfth; at the second, sixth. He said afterwards that his
mind was concentrated on attacking the bottom third of
the course; and that was where he now won the gold
medal and his place in history.*

OLYMPIC HISTORY FOR TOMBA

Page 136
The Japanese take their first gold medal in the Games in the Nordic combined by holding off the Norwegians and the Austrians.

Deborah Compagnoni: a golden day for Italy.

They say that 10,000 Italians crossed the Alps to be present at Val d'Isère and demonstrate their adulation for La Bomba. The trip was worth it, in every way. Alberto Tomba created Olympic history by becoming the first successfully to defend an Alpine title. And he did so in the most dramatic manner possible, snatching victory with the fastest time of the day as the last of the 15 seeded skiers in the Giant Slalom. By a 0.32 seconds margin over the two runs, he denied Marc Girardelli, his fiercest rival, the gold medal.

Now these two fine skiers were left to dispute the slalom title four days later at Les Menuires, with Tomba, one of the most extrovert showmen we have Known, attempting a "double double". A hero from a city, Bologna, rather than a conventional mountain background, Tomba had confirmed his position as the most prominent sportsman in all of Italy, acclaimed more than any footballer. «I didn't know I had won until I saw the flags waving» Tomba said afterwards, playing to the emotion of his fanatical followers. The delay

in finding out would not have been much more than the margin of his victory.

Seldom has a race been so dominated by the two favourites. Tomba set the pace on the first run, a mere 0.13 secs faster than Girardelli, the skier who quit his native Austria as a boy, under the influence of his father, following a dispute with the national ski federation. Ever since, Girardelli has ploughed a lonely furrow under the flag of Luxembourg. Flags were nothing against personal rivalry, as the two men carved their way through the gates.

The tension was electric among the crowd as Girardelli took the lead on the second run ahead of Kjetil Aamodt of Norway, already the winner of the Super-G and now taking the bronze. The demand on Tomba could not have been more extreme; like a champion he met it. None can know how much he was helped by consultation with a psychologist during his relative decline between Calgary and Albertville.

Maybe it was simply the adrenalin that the Olympic Games generate in a great competitor. At the first interval-

time on the second run Tomba was twelfth; at the second, sixth. He said afterwards that his mind was concentrated on attacking the bottom third of the course; and that was where he now won the gold medal and his place in history.

It was a day of double celebration for Italy. Deborah Compagnoni, inevitably nick-named "Tombagnoni" in reflection of a comparable style, had the audacity to defeat Carole Merle, the Super-G home favourite. Her commanding run at Méribel came a short time before Tomba's ultimate piece of mastery, fifty kilometres distant.

In a different way, it was a sterling performance by Compagnoni, who a year ago had major intestinal surgery and suffers intermittent pains. Already, on this moment that happens only once every four years, some of the world's best skiers had tried and failed to match the time set by Merle; Petra Kronberger of Austria, Katja Seizinger of Germany, and Ulrike Maier of Austria. Compagnoni, despite her pains, flew down the hill a substantial 1.41 secs faster than Merle, who holds nine World Cup victories and was runner-up in last years World Championship. Now Merle was left with reflections that will never become any easier to accept. That is sport. Only Compagnoni knows the true extent of her own courage.

At Courchevel, Japan won its first medal in the Winter Olympics for twenty years, when the men's Nordic combined team held off Norway and Austria in the 3x10 kilometre relay. The Japanese had a substantial lead from the ski jumping, and sustained their efforts across the slopes, finishing almost a minute and a half ahead of Norway. In the 4x10 kilometre relay at Les Saisies, Norway remained dominant, and Vegard Ulveng, skiing the second leg, became the leading medal winner of the Games with three golds and a silver.

France's run in the ice-hockey came to an end against the United States, in a quarter-final that closed with a free-for-all punch-up between all the players from both camps. The U.S.A. had won 4-1, after being a goal down in the first period. Ray LeBlanc, in goal, was once more than Americans'

key figure; but rough tactics by their defenders, four of whom incurred two-minute penalties late in the third period, provoked the disorderly confrontation at the end of time. A partisan French crowd howled their disapproval.

Apeland guides the Norwegian team to silver in the Nordic combined.

Cry of joy from Jari Isometsa, Finland.

Pages 140-141
Michaela Gerg, Germany, eighth in the Super-G.

139

Page 142-143
Tomba La Bomba repeats the Olympic title in Giant Slalom he won in Calgary.

The Norwegians , their king present, exult. Bjorn Daehlie, in the picture, celebrates the win in the relay.

Page 145
A view of the men's 1,000m speed skating, won by the German Olaf Zinke.

DAY

12

There is a reflection of life itself
in the brutality with which misfortune strikes down
some, while others are favoured;
and we never know how much these variations lie
within the mental framework of the competitors
themselves. There *is the fascination.*

SUNNY GIRL FROM SWEDEN

Midori Ito, JPN, on her way to a medal.

Page 146
Czechoslovakia/Finland

art of the beauty of the Olympic Games, of their unique position, comes not from abstract and ethical considerations, but from simple numerical infrequency. World championships are one thing: the Olympics another. There is a reflection of life itself in the brutality with which misfortune strikes down some, while others are favoured; and we never know how much these variations lie within the mental framework of the competitors themselves. *There* is the fascination. On the twelfth day of the Games in Albertville, the figure of the moment was a smiling, sunny girl from Sweden, Pernilla Wiberg, winning for her country its first ever women's Alpine medal.

Most eyes at the Giant Slalom at Méribel had been turned in other directions: towards Schneider of Switzerland, and Kronberger and Wachter of Austria, to Merle of France and Roffe of America. Or Compagnoni, champion of the Super-G the day before. Yet it was Wiberg, laden with criticism at home all season on account of mediocre performances, who now came good on the day that will live with her for ever. Being world champion could not compare with this.

She started well. On the first of the two runs, she lay second behind Ulrike Maier of Austria. Carole Merle, hoping so fervently to make good her disappointment from the Super-G, lay fourth, half a second behind Maier. Yet something was missing, on her own admission, from Merle's disposition on these vital two days, and she would finish sixth.

Schneider, Kronberger and Compagnoni had gone, all failing to complete the run, Compagnoni twisting a knee that would need further operation. The field had been thinned. On the second run, Diann Roffe faultlessly swept down the course, to leap from ninth position to tie for the silver medal with Anita Wachter. But it was Wiberg, with marvellous consistency and a second run a mere 0.02 seconds slower than her first, who found fame and history.

For the United States, less than happy at this stage of the Games with its overall position among the medals of seventh, there was the satisfaction of Roffe's silver — after years of set-back through injuries — and fifth and seventh place respectively for Julie Tarlslen and Eva Twardokens.

For more than a century, since before the rebirth of the Games, women have been campaigning for equality with men. Nowhere has that been more difficult than in sport, on account of the superior physical strength of men, and an undefined but perceived temperamental superiority. If one event has helped to shift that perception, it has been the introduction of the women's biathlon, with its extreme demands of physical and mental endurance.

The winner of the women's 15 kilometre event — following the 7.5k and relay events — was Antje Misersky of Germany, her third medal in all. She finished over eleven seconds ahead of Svetlana Pecherskaia of the Unified Team, with Myriam Bedard of Canada in third place. The Games of 1992 were particularly notable for the women of France, in several disciplines, never mind the sorrow of Merle. In the Biathlon relay they had taken the gold medal, and now Véronique Claudel, Delphine Burlet and Corinne Niogret earned an unofficial "team" medal in the 15k with their respective fourth, sixth and seventh positions.

At ice-hockey, the Unified Team swept aside Finland, by six goals to one, to set up the semi-final, between former ideological rivals, against the United States, with its echoes of 1980. In the preliminary rounds of the short-track speed skating, admitted as full medal sport for the first time, Michael Daignault of Canada overshadowed the world champion, Wilf O'Reilly of Britain, with the fastest time over 1,000 metres of 1min 33.21secs.

Short track speedskating, an official sport at the Olympic Games for the first time.

A broken ski pole prevented Vreni Schneider, Switzerland, from continuing her downhill.

Fine haul for the American women in giant slalom. Here, Julie Parisien, 5th.

Pernila Wiberg: a surprise for Sweden.

The Australian Sandra Paintin, 40th in the 15km of the women's biathlon.

Following pages:
In the ice hall in Pralognan, Great Britain beats Japan 10-3 in curling, a demonstration sport.

Following pages:
Mont-Blanc in the background, 45 men and 20 women train at 200 km/h in Les Arcs 2000.

DAY

13

If the champion was Kronberger, the story was Coberger. Petra Kronberger of Austria ended the Winter Games as she began them, adding the Slalom title on the last day of Alpine skiing to the Combined event she had won on the opening day of the women's events.

NEW ZEALANDER MAKES NEWS

If the champion was Kronberger, the *story* was Coberger. Petra Kronberger of Austria ended the Winter Games as she began them, adding the Slalom title on the last day of Alpine skiing to the Combined event she had won on the opening day of the women's events. It proved her the outstanding competitor of her discipline; yet a new page was being written in Olympic history with the silver medal of Annelise Coberger of New Zealand. No competitor from the southern hemisphere, let alone New Zealand, had ever previously won a medal at the Winter Games.

Coberger, 20, had given intimations of her potential on the World Cup circuit, winning one event in Austria and having two third places. Her father runs a ski-shop in Christchurch. Lying eight after the first run at Méribel, Coberger leaped to second place with the fastest time of 44.08 seconds on the second run. "I had nothing to lose, so I just went for it" she said afterwards.

A quarter of a second behind Coberger was Blanca Fernandez-Ochoa, of Spain, whose elder brother Francisco won the slalom at Sapporo in 1972 when she was eight. A serious injury during the Calgary Games had threatened her career. Leading on the first run was Julie Parisien of the U.S.A., fractions ahead of Kronberger and Vreni Schneider, Switzerland's last hope of a skiing medal. On the second

run, Parisien faded to eighth, fourth overall by 0.05secs, and Schneider to seventh over the two runs.

Another outsider to make the headlines was Evgeni Redkine, a 22-year-old of the Unified Team, selected at the last moment for the 20-kilometre biathlon and not to be found on the Olympic data-bank. Until he won. Mark Kirchner of Germany had been optimistic of a clean sweep of biathlon medals, but Redkine did not miss one of the 20 shooting targets, and Kirchner had to accept the silver medal some six seconds, adrift, after incurring a three-minute penalty. Mikael Lofgren of Sweden took the bronze.

Another New Zealander with a chance of a medal was the 27-year-old Mike McMillen, who reached the four-man final of the Short-track speed skating 1,000 metres. The three rounds on the final night of this new full-medal sport were packed with drama and produced two world records. Considering that the programme of the Winter Games is lean on some days, there is surely a sound basis for widening the available number of individual events in this lively sport.

McMillen, tall for a sport that requires a low centre of gravity on the eighteen sharp bends of the kilometre race, was second in both his quarter- and semi-finals to Koreans: Ki-Hoon Kim and Joon-Ho Lee respectively. The semi-final was doubly memorable: Lee set a record of 1min 31.27secs, and Wilf O'Reilly of Britain, the world champion of 1991, crashed out on the first bend of the sixth lap. O'Reilly was accelerating off the bend, attempting to hold off McMillen as the New Zealander tried to overtake. There was a slight collision, but O'Reilly said that "there was no injustice". This is a cut-throat sport: not in mentality, but on account of the proximity of the racers at high speed on a small circuit.

In the final, McMillen took an early lead, than gave way to Kim. For three laps McMillen was at his shoulder, but was passed on the last two laps by both Fred Blackburn, a 19-year-old Canadian, and Lee. Kim, from Seoul, further improved the record to 1:30.76. O'Reilly, who had won both the 500 and 1,000 demonstration events at Calgary, earned fifth place by winning the B final.

There was an upset in the open-air speed skating when Bart Veldkamp of Holland beat Johann-Olav Koss, the Norwegian world record-holder, by almost three seconds, Geir Karlstad of Norway finishing third. Dutch klaxons were rending the night air of Albertville as the newly arriving spectators took their indoor seats for the adjacent short-track.

Josh Thompson of the USA concentrating hard in the men's 20km biathlon.

Pages 160-161:
Annelise Coberger of New Zealand fences with the posts.

John Mueller training flat out
for the speed-skiing.

Light play on Albertville's speedskating rink during the men's 10,000m.

Pages 164-165:
The Canadians take the gold in the women's 3,000m short-track speedskating.

DAY

Some of the women in the Games in Albertville
have taught the men a lesson: that it is possible to be
successful and at the same time not take
yourself too seriously.

END OF THE ROAD FOR LeBlanc

Page 166
Surya Bonaly's «corrida» was not enough for a place on the podium.

The Unified Team's bob glides in the first run along a course that has been perfectly prepared.

There were times in the ice-hockey semi-final between the Unified Team and the United States when it seemed that there was only one team out there on the rink...The former Soviets would click the puck back and forth across the ice, man to man, sometimes retaining possession for twenty passes at a time, as though enjoying a private practice. It proved to be the end of the line for Ray LeBlanc, the American goalkeeper, whose defiant exploits had done so much to take his team so far. But as Igor Dmitriev, the United Team's deputy coach, reflected afterwards: «The outcome of a match is based on an entire team, not just the goalkeeper.»

The story of the semi-final is simply told by the statistics: LeBlanc had to fend off three times as many shots as his opposite number over the whole match, and almost five times as many during the third period. With the score misleadingly balanced at 2-2 at the end of the second period, the Unified Team having been 2-1 ahead, three goals in the third period sank the United States, ending

their dream of a third gold medal in the sport, following 1960 and 1980.

The style of the American team maintained the pattern of their tournament: defensive and physical. They suffered five two-minute penalties in the third period, and no team could hope to survive such a handicap against the experts from the Commonwealth of Independent States. The United States was unhappy with some of the decisions of the Swedish referee - what referee ever pleased both sides in a team sport? - but their coach Dave Peterson was generous to the victors. «A very fine team» he reflected.

The Unified Team was only one goal ahead with six minutes remaining, and then Khmylev and Davydov put them beyond reach. For the ninth time in ten Olympic hockey tournaments, the Russian Republics would be competing for not less than a silver medal when they met Canada, victors over Czechoslovakia in the other semi-final.

Three medals for Stefania Belmondo: Italy rejoices!

Some of the women in the Games in Albertville have taught the men a lesson: that it is possible to be successful and at the same time not take yourself too seriously. Coberger of New Zealand, Wiberg of Sweden, Compagnoni of Italy and now Stefania Belmondo, also of Italy, allowed their finest hour to be as soothing as a thermal bath, instead of feeling obliged to say through clenched teeth «This is my greatest moment». Some occasions do not need the most obvious words.

Belmondo had previously won a silver and a bronze in earlier races - this was the first Olympics with five nordic races for women - and now her gold in the 30-kilometre event made her Italy's leading medallist of these Games. Yet the two Unified Team skiers behind her, Lyubov Egorova and Elena Valbe, became the first women to win five medals in a single Winter Games. The only man to have done so was Eric Heiden of the U.S.A., with all speed skating golds in 1980. Egorova had three golds and two silvers, Valbe one gold and four bronzes. Belmondo, who set a blistering pace to win by twelve seconds in 1hr 22mins 30.1secs, was supported at Les Saisies by many of the villagers from her tiny hamlet of Pietrapoprio in Piedmonte.

Randy, Joseph, Karlos and Christopher go for it.

There was another anti-climax for the host country on the figure skating rink in Albertville, this time in the women's event. As in the ice dancing, it was apparent prior to the free-style programme that the leading French candidate, in this instance the appealing Surya Bonaly, was unlikely to climb among the medals. So it proved. Kristi Yamaguchi of the United States, who had led on the Original programme, fully justified her world championship title from 1991. There is a lissom, unextended quality about

her style, and she ably followed in the line of previous American winners, Albright (1956), Heiss (1960), Fleming (1968) and Hamill (1976).

So much of Bonaly's impact depended on her muscularly impressive jumps: but she failed in an attempted quadruple toe-loop and finished fifth. Midori Ito of Japan, fourth on the Original programme, spun her way to the silver medal. Nancy Kerrigan (US) was third.

The Unified Team showed the
Americans a few things. The
final score in Méribel was 5-2.

After her world title in Munich, gold for Kristi Yamaguchi in Albertville.

Lenka Kulovana of Czecho-slovakia, with a daring free programme.

DAY 15

«I could have saved maybe half a second on the first run,
nothing exceptional» he reflected. «The silver
medal is good, I have no special regrets. Near the bottom
of the first run, following mistakes, it crossed my mind to
quit... and then I thought, this is the Olympics!»

TOMBA UPSTAGED BY JAGGE

Page 174
The Jamaica-I bob curves in
high on the turn.

After a seven-year absence from
competition, Cathy Turner wins
the women's 500m short track
speedskating.

Alpine skiing is the flag bearer of the Winter Games: determined by absolute measurement, visually spectacular and artistic, technically demanding in the extreme, seldom without danger or risk of injury. The final event, the men's slalom at Les Menuires, epitomised all; and added to it the element of surprise. Alberto Tomba failed to repeat his defense of the title held from Calgary, outpaced by Finn Christian Jagge from Norway. This was a doubly memorable day for Norway, who rose to second place in the medals table behind Germany, and ahead of the Unified Team by two, with only the hockey final to be decided.

The gold medal was effectively destined for Jagge on the first run. Skiing brilliantly for the fastest time of 51.43secs, he was a huge 1.58secs ahead of Tomba, lying sixth. Jagge was over a second ahead of the second fastest, Michael Tritscher of Austria, who would take the bronze medal. Could Tomba possibly close such a gap on the second run?

His effort was worthy of a champion, but not enough: although Jagge was this time sixth fastest, he maintained the overall lead by 0.28secs. Tomba had overhauled Staub and Accola of Switzerland, Fogdoe of Sweden and Tritscher, but had to be content with a silver medal.

Tomba was one of the first to congratulate Jagge, but revealed afterwards - to what degree self-defensively we cannot know - that he considered he and his ski-technician

had wrongly prepared the skis for that course. «I could have saved maybe half a second on the first run, nothing exceptional» he reflected. «The silver medal is good, I have no special regrets. Near the bottom of the first run, following mistakes, it crossed my mind to quit... and then I thought, this is the Olympics!»

Bob-sleigh is a minority sport under pressure from the factors of both expense and ecology, but big crowds gathered at La Plagne for the two days of the four-man event, dominated predictably by Germany, Switzerland and Austria. The acclaim of the second day was for Ingo Appelt, driver of Austria-1, which had been 0.07 seconds behind the famous Wolfgang Hoppe in Germany-1 after the first two runs. In a see-saw battle, Appelt took the third run, in first place, 0.16 ahead of Hoppe in seventh position. On the final run, Hoppe was second, Appelt third; and the gold was Austria's by 0.02secs, less than the flick of an eye-lid. Gustav Weder, another doyen of the sport, led Switzerland to the bronze by overhauling Canada-1.

There really was no holding Norway in these Games. While Jagge was breaking the Alpine mould, Bjorn Daehlie was winning the men's 50 kilometre cross-country at Les Saisies, ahead of the Italians Maurillo de Zolt and Giorgio Vanzetta. Although Daehlie had nearly a minute in hand, winning in 2hrs 3mins 41.5secs, he was almost passing out with exhaustion on the final uphill section, where thousands of Italian spectators were roaring home their men. The silver medal was particularly sweet for de Zolt in his forty third year.

No new arrival has made a better impression than short-track speed skating; and the women's 500 metres final had all the tension, following a recall for a fall in the first twenty metres, of a Summer Olympics track sprint. In a photo-finish, the two racers having bumped as they came off the final bend, Cathy Turner of the United States was given the verdict over Yan Li of China by 0.04secs. It was Turner who had crashed in the frenzied (start, so she was fortunate for the re-call); an astonishing climax after having

Victory is elusive for Tomba, who receives the silver.

Bjorn Daehlie: total, but golden, exhaustion.

retired from the sport eleven years ago, and making a come-back after watching the finals at Calgary.

In the bronze medal match for the ice-hockey, Czechoslovakia, so long a force in the sport — silver medallists in 1948, 1968, 1976, 1984, bronze in 1920, 1964 and 1972 — crushed the United States by six goals to one.

The demonstration event of speed skiing, indeed the entire Games, was in mourning for the death of Nicholas Bochatay, the Swiss skier who died following an accident in training shortly before the final, in which he was to have competed. Bochatay had been thirteenth among the semi-final qualifiers the previous day.

His death brought into focus that element of the Games that tends to be overlooked: that medal winners, the headlines, the million-dolar sponsorships, are all as nothing without the thousands of competitors who are there to create the whole, to try to fulfil their private ambition, however small. Bochatay had been a promising Swiss junior, until a knee injury eight years ago curtailed his ambitions. So he carried on with his carpentry at the family business at Martigny, and turned his attention to speed skiing, becoming national champion. The day before he had broken his personal record with 210.65kph. His sport had helped give him a life, and now took it away from him.

The presidents of the IOC and the organising committee of the Games, Juan Antonio Samaranch, Michel Barnier and Jean-Claude Killy, immediately flew to Les Arcs upon news of the tragedy. A minute's silence was observed at the awards ceremony, the victors having been the favourites: Michel Prufer of France, a doctor at Grenoble, with a speed of 229.299kph, and Tarja Mulari of Finland at 219.245kph. Both times were new world records.

First gold medal in bob for the Austrians.

Page 179
James Morgan launches forward

Page 181
Second gold of the day for the Norwegians, thanks to Finn-Christian Jagge.

Resounding defeat for the Americans against the Czechoslovaks, 1-6.

In Pralognan-la-Vanoise, the Swiss win the curling final 7-6.

DAY
16

A concluding firework display had explosions loud
enough, it seemed, to have started avalanches at the
distant sites. Finally, the compère invited audience and
athletes to join together in the arena to dance the polka.
In a thousand ways, we would remember the first
French Games for twenty four years.

A Milestone in History

The XVI Olympic Winter Games came to a close in Albertville with a ceremony as elegant, and eloquent, as that with which they had begun sixteen days earlier. They arrived, and departed, with style. And they had proved to be a milestone in the history of the Olympic Movement. Jean-Claude Killy and Michel Barnier, the co-presidents, and their organising committee, had demonstrated that the Games in Savoie, a *regional* Games, could succeed. They had been accomplished without discernible flaw.

Many people had not believed that it could be done, that an Olympics spread over thirteen different competition sites would be too broad a task for management. Yet with a transport system more complex than any previously attempted, the network was held together. More than that, in collaboration with the six international winter sports federations, the competitions were staged with theatrical efficiency. The Games in Albertville shone in continuous fine weather, and the few snow-storms failed to disrupt the co-ordination.

Some, admittedly, found the travelling arduous. That was bound to be so once the International Olympic Committee had voted for Savoie in 1986 and accepted the multiplicity of sites. Yet as Juan Antonio Samaranch, the IOC President observed: «These Games were finer than we could have hoped. The French know their winter sports so well, and all the events were first class. The only problem was the many hours spent travelling, although we had always known that there were many sites.»

The French adroitly used the various famous sports resorts at their disposal, and they set a precedent for what the President had proposed, the possibility of Games

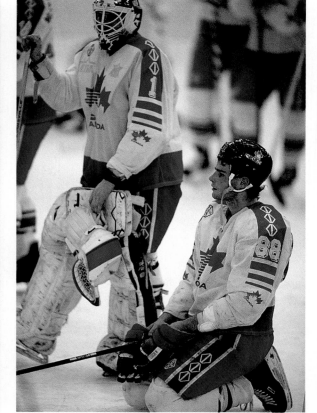

Eric Lindros on his knees, the Canadians beaten 1-3 in the final by the Unified Team.

186

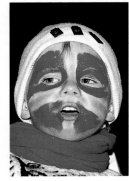

shared by different countries. Before the XVI Games had ended there was talk of a Winter Games bid jointly by Austria, Italy and Slovenia in their eastern corner of the Alps. The caution must be that Games too widely spread detract from that basic ethic: the unity of the youth of the world. The competitors of an Olympics must not become isolated from each other.

The Games were a milestone in another sense. When the Unified Team, the former Soviet Union, beat Canada by three goals to one in the ice-hockey final, it was the last hurrah of a formidable force that has dominated Olympic sport for forty years. The Russian Republic, stretching from the Baltic shores to the east of Asia, and Ukraine will continue to field powerful teams, but the Olympic panorama will never be quite the same again. In my opinion, the Games were better without that traditional mock-ideological warfare between the USSR and USA. It was thrilling to see

the rise of Norway, especially in Alpine events; and therein was a lesson for all. Norway's climb in the medal table was not due to the quality of its competitors so much as improvement in coaching. The emerging countries, of Asia, Africa and elsewhere, must concentrate on education in sport as much as the simple funding of athletes.

Title and final gold of the sixteenth Olympic Winter Games for the Unified Team.

Norway's national joy was as notable as the unaccustomed and hard-to-explain failure of Switzerland, one of the foremost winter sports nations.

The newly-arrived NOCs - the Baltic states, Croatia and Slovenia - may not have won medals but they celebrated their presence, the raising of their flags. Whatever the original philosophy of de Coubertin, national pride is an inseparable motive force within the Olympic movement. More than two hundred of Slovenia's population of two million made the twelve-hour drive to Courchevel, on the second Sunday of the Games, for the ski jumping event, to witness Franci Petek finish eighth. Croatia had competitors

in the first 30 in figure skating, Latvia finished inside the top twenty in bobsled, Estonia had a fourteen-year-old girl. Olga Vassiljeva, distinguish herself in the figure skating. For all the peoples of the world, the Olympic Games are a path to identity.

France once more brought its own identity unmistakably to the closing ceremony: a cavalcade of colour, costume, music and dance. Leading performers - Paul Duchesnay for the hosts - paraded the national flags again, the Mayor of Albertville passed the Olympic flag to the Mayor of Lillehammer, the host city of 1994 Olympic Winter Games, and Juan Antonio Samaranch bestowed upon Barnier and

Killy the Olympic gold order.

There followed an ice-dance intermingled with circus acts, performed with an informal abandon that is quintessentially French. There was folk dancing in local costume, together with enchanting children, and an accordion band even brought along their dog. A concluding firework display had explosions loud enough, it seemed, to have started avalanches at the distant sites. Finally, the compère invited audience and athletes to join together in the arena to dance the polka. In a thousand ways, we would remember the first French Games for twenty four years.

Albertville '92 Olympic Winter Games in Facts and Figures

THE PROGRAMME:
The Olympic programme included 12 sports:
Alpine Skiing
Bobsleigh
Biathlon
Cross Country Skiing
Figure Skating
Luge
Ice Hockey
Nordic Combined
Ski Jump
Speed Skating
Short Track Speed Skating
Freestyle Skiing (Moguls)

as well as three demonstration sports:
Curling
Speed Skiing
Freestyle Skiing (Ballet and Aerials)
In total, 57 Olympic and 8 demonstration events took place over 16 days.
330 medals were awarded.

TRANSPORTATION
A total of 3,100 vehicles were used by 2,750 drivers:
1,550 buses with 1,700 drivers
1,500 cars with 1,000 drivers
50 trucks with 50 drivers

COMPUTERS
1,800 IBM personal computers were used by the Olympic Family within the most advanced information system.

The organizing Committee produced:
1,500 different result reports
2,500 different world press agency reports
50,000 messages were exchanged

PRESS, TV AND INFORMATION
A total of 7,407 media accreditations were issued for the Games:
Written press and photographers:
1,325 journalists (1,196 men and 129 women)
525 photographers (499 men and 26 women)
170 technicians
Electronic media:
Host broadcaster: 1,722
World broadcasters: 3,609
320 hours of the international TV signal were produced, with:
176 fixed TV cameras
250 Electronic News Gathering crews
560 commentator's booths
400 photocopiers made a total of 20 million copies during the Games.
KODAK laboratories processed more than 80,000 rolls of films in three laboratories (La Léchère, Val d'Isère et Les Saisies).
135 collaborators, from 13 different countries,
including 56 Savoyards, worked 20 hours/day.

In Albertville was presented for the first time the Electronic Imageria with digital camera and the transmission service, free of charge for accredited photographers.

For KODAK, this was the largest Operation ever run.

PARTICIPANTS

A record number of 64 National Olympic
Committees attended the Games.
A TOTAL OF 37,721 ACCREDITATIONS WERE
ISSUED!
2,147 athletes (1,545 men and 602 women)
were accompanied by 1,843 officials.
8,000 volunteers, members of the "Team"92"
worked during the Games.
The youngest athlete: Krisztina CZAKO
(HUN),figure skating, was born on December
17th, 1978.
The oldest athlete: Kalevi HAKKINEN (FIN),
speedskiing, is just 64 years old.
The heaviest athlete: Jan LANGEVELD (NED),
two-man bobsled, 115 kg.
The lightest athlete: Line HADDAD (FRA),
figure skating pairs,
35 kg.

The tallest athlete: Raymond LeBlanc and
Maurice MANTHA, both in the USA ice-hockey team, 2m10.
The smallest athlete: Midori ITO (JPN),
silver medallist in figure skating, 1m45.

SECURITY

7,800 police officers, soldiers and firefighters
ensured the security of the Games.

FOOD

In the official restaurants, 2,300,000 meals
were served on 120,000 plates, using 180,000
glasses and 700,000 sets of cutlery.
The participants consumed:
20,000 kg of beef
26,000 kg of cheese
800,000 bread rolls
300,000 "baguettes"

DOWNHILL MEN

1.	ORTLIEB P.	AUT	1:50.37
2.	PICCARD F.	FRA	1:50.42
3.	MADER G.	AUT	1:50.47
4.	WASMEIER M.	GER	1:50.62
5.	THORSEN J.E.	NOR	1:50.79
6.	HEINZER F.	SUI	1:51.39
7.	TAUSCHER H.	GER	1:51.49
8.	ARNESEN L.	NOR	1:51.63
9.	KITT A.J.	USA	1:51.98
10.	COLTURI F.	ITA	1:52.07

COMBINED COMPETITION MEN

1.	POLIG J.	ITA	14.58 points
2.	MARTIN G.	ITA	14.90 points
3.	LOCHER S.	SUI	18.16 points
4.	CRETIER J.L.	FRA	18.97 points
5.	WASMEIER M.	GER	32.77 points
6.	GHEDINA K.	ITA	38.96 points
7.	FURUSETH O.C.	NOR	40.47 points
8.	GIGANDET X.	SUI	41.21 points
9.	ISHIOKA T.	JPN	51.83 points
10.	ARNESEN L.	NOR	51.93 points

SUPER-G MEN

1.	AAMODT K.A.	NOR	1:13.04
2.	GIRARDELLI M.	LUX	1:13.77
3.	THORSEN J.E.	NOR	1:13.83
4.	FURUSETH O.C.	NOR	1:13.87
5.	POLIG J.	ITA	1:13.88
6.	HANGL M.	SUI	1:13.90
7.	MADER G.	AUT	1:14.08
8.	STIANSENT.	NOR	1:14.51
9.	WASMEIER M.	GER	1:14.58
10.	ACCOLA P.	SUI	1:14.60

GIANT SLALOM MEN

1.	TOMBA A.	ITA	2:06.98
2.	GIRARDELLI M.	LUX	2:07.30
3.	AAMODT K.A.	NOR	2:07.82
4.	ACCOLA P.	SUI	2:08.02
5.	FURUSETH O.C.	NOR	2:08.16
6.	MADER G.	AUT	2:08.80
7.	SALZGEBER R.	AUT	2:08.83
8.	NYBERG F.	SWE	2:09.00
9.	STROLZ H.	AUT	2:09.45
9.	POLIG J.	ITA	2:09.45

SLALOM MEN

1.	JAGGE F.C.	NOR	1:44.39
2.	TOMBA A.	ITA	1:44.67
3.	TRITSCHER M.	AUT	1:44.85
4.	STAUB P.	SUI	1:45.44
5.	FOGDOE T.	SWE	1:45.48
6.	ACCOLA P.	SUI	1:45.62
7.	VON GRUENIGEN M.	SUI	1:46.42
8.	NILSSON J.	SWE	1:46.57
9.	STANGASSINGER T.	AUT	1:46.65
10.	GROSJEAN M.	USA	1:46.94

COMBINED COMPETITION LADIES

1.	KRONBERGER P.	AUT	2.55 points
2.	WACHTER A.	AUT	19.39 points
3.	MASNADA F.	FRA	21.38 points
4.	BOURNISSEN C.	SUI	24.98 points
5.	BERGE A.	NOR	35.28 points
6.	MCKENDRY M.	CAN	39.02 points
7.	BOKAL N.	SLO	42.60 points
8.	MEDZIHRADSKA L.	TCH	47.43 points
9.	VOGT M.	GER	48.52 points
10.	CAVAGNOUD R.	FRA	51.13 points

DOWNHILL LADIES

1.	LEE-GARTNER K.	CAN	1:52.55
2.	LINDH H.	USA	1:52.61
3.	WALLINGER V.	AUT	1:52.64
4.	SEIZINGER K.	GER	1:52.67
5.	KRONBERGER P.	AUT	1:52.73
6.	GUTENSOHN K.	GER	1:53.71
7.	SADLEDER B.	AUT	1:53.81
8.	GLADISHIVA S.	EUN	1:53.85
9.	VOGT M.	GER	1:53.89
10.	ZURBRIGGEN H.	SUI	1:54.04

SUPER-G LADIES

1.	COMPAGNONI D.	ITA	1:21.22
2.	MERLE C.	FRA	1:22.63
3.	SEIZINGER K.	GER	1:23.19
4.	KRONBERGER P.	AUT	1:23.20
5.	MAIER U.	AUT	1:23.35
6.	LEE-GARTNER K.	CAN	1:23.76
7.	GERG M.	GER	1:23.77
8.	TWARDOKENS E.	USA	1:24.19
9.	WACHTER A.	AUT	1:24.20
10.	HAAS Z.	SUI	1:24.31

GIANT SLALOM LADIES

1.	WIBERG P.	SWE	2:12.74
2.	ROFFE D.	USA	2:13.71
2.	WACHTER A.	AUT	2:13.71
4.	MAIER U.	AUT	2:13.77
5.	PARISIEN J.	USA	2:14.10
6.	MERLE C.	FRA	2:14.24
7.	TWARDOKENS E.	USA	2:14.47
8.	SEIZINGER K.	GER	2:14.96
9.	EDER S.	AUT	2:15.05
10.	ANDERSSON K.	SWE	2:15.23

SLALOM LADIES

1.	KRONBERGER P.	AUT	1:32.68
2.	COBERGER A.	NZL	1:33.10
3.	FERNANDEZ OCHOA B.	ESP	1:33.35
4.	PARISIEN J.	USA	1:33.40
5.	BUDER K.	AUT	1:33.68
6.	CHAUVET P.	FRA	1:33.72
7.	SCHNEIDER V.	SUI	1:33.96
8.	BERGE A.	NOR	1:34.22
9.	NEUENSCHWANDER K.	SUI	1:34.28
10.	HROVAT U.	SLO	1:34.50

MOGULS - LADIES

1. WEINBRECHT D.	USA	23.69 points
2. KOJEVNIKOVA E.	EUN	23.50 points
3. HATTESTAD S.	NOR	23.04 points
4. MITTERMAYER T.	GER	22.33 points
5. STEIN B.	GER	21.44 points
6. MCINTYRE L.	USA	21.24 points
7. MARCIANDI S.	ITA	19.66 points
8. MONOD R.	FRA	15.57 points

MOGULS - MEN

1. GROSPIRON E.	FRA	25.81 points
2. ALLAMAND O.	FRA	24.87 points
3. CARMICHAEL N.	USA	24.82 points
4. BERTHON E.	FRA	24.79 points
5. SMART J.	CAN	24.15 points
6. PAAJARVI J.	SWE	24.14 points
7. BRASSARD J.-L.	CAN	23.71 points
8. PERSSON L.	SWE	22.99 points
9. GILG Y.	FRA	22.85 points
10. BINER J.	SUI	22.69 points

CROSS COUNTRY SKIING LADIES, 10 km FREE - PURSUIT

1. EGOROVA L.	EUN	40:07.7
2. BELMONDO S.	ITA	40:31.8
3. VALBE E.	EUN	40:51.7
4. LUKKARINEN M.	FIN	41:05.1
5. NILSEN E.	NOR	41:26.9
6. WESTIN M.H.	SWE	41:28.2
7. NYBRATEN I.H.	NOR	41:35.1
8. LASUTINA L.	EUN	41:48.8
9. MANCINI I.	FRA	41:53.3
10. DI CENTA M.	ITA	42:09.7

CROSS COUNTRY SKIING LADIES, 5km CLASSICAL - PURSUIT

1. LUKKARINEN M.	FIN	14:13.8
2. EGOROVA L.	EUN	14:14.7
3. VALBE E.	EUN	14:22.7
4. BELMONDO S.	ITA	14:26.2
5. NYBRATEN I.H.	NOR	14:33.3
6. DANILOVA O.	EUN	14:37.2
7. LASUTINA L.	EUN	14:41.7
8. PEDERSEN S.	NOR	14:42.1
9. WESTIN M.H.	SWE	14:42.6
10. NILSEN E.	NOR	14:50.8

CROSS COUNTRY SKIING LADIES, 15km CLASSICAL

1. EGOROVA L.	EUN	42:20.8
2. LUKKARINEN M.	FIN	43:29.9
3. VALBE E.	EUN	43:42.3
4. Smetanina R.	EUN	44:01.5
5. Belmondo S.	ITA	44:02.4
6. Kirvesniemi M.L.	FI	44:02.7
7. Nybraten I.H.	NOR	44:18.6
8. Dybendahl T.	NOR	44:31.5
9. Paruzzi G.	ITA	44:44.0
10. Westin M.H.	SWE	45:00.5

CROSS COUNTRY SKIING LADIES, RELAY 4x5km MIX

1. VALBE E.	EUN	59:34.8
SMETANINA R.		
LASUTINA L.		
EGOROVA L.		
2. PEDERSEN S.	NOR	59:56.4
NYBRATEN I.H.		
DYBENDAHL T.		
NILSEN E.		
3. VANZETTA B.	ITA	1:00:25.9
DI CENTA M.		
PARUZZI G.		
BELMONDO S.		
4. KIRVESNIEMI M.L.	FIN	1:00:52.9
MAATTA P.		
SAVOLAINEN J.		
LUKKARINEN M.		
5. STANISIERE C.	FRA	1:01:30.7
GIRY ROUSSET S.		
VILLENEUVE S.		
MANCINI I.		
6. BALAZOVA L.	TCH	1:01:37.4
NEUMANOVA K.		
HAVRANCIKOVA A.		
ZELINGEROVA I.		
7. GORLIN C.	SWE	1:01:54.5
WALLIN M.		
SATERKVIST K.		
WESTIN M.H.		
8. WEZEL H.	GER	1:02:22.6
HESS G.		
OPITZ S.		
KUMMEL I.		
9. HONEGGER S.	SUI	1:02:54.1
ALBRECHT B.		
LEONARDI N.		
KNECHT E.		
10. RUCHALA M.	POL	1:03:23.0
KWASNA D.		
BOCEK B.		
NOWAK H.		

CROSS COUNTRY SKIING LADIES, 30km FREE TECHNIQUE

1. BELMONDO S.	ITA	1:22:30.1
2. EGOROVA L.	EUN	1:22:52.0
3. VALBE E.	EUN	1:24:13.9
4. NILSEN E.	NOR	1:26:25.1
5. LASUTINA L.	EUN	1:26:31.8
6. DI CENTA M.	ITA	1:27:04.4
7. WESTIN M.-H.	SWE	1:27:16.2
8. OPITZ S.	GER	1:27:17.4
9. DYBENDAHL T.	NOR	1:27:29.8
10. LUKKARINEN M.	FIN	1:27:30.9

CROSS COUNTRY SKIING MEN, 30km CLASSICAL

1. ULVANG V.	NOR	1:22:27.8
2. DAEHLIE B.	NOR	1:23:14.0
3. LANGLI T.	NOR	1:23:42.5
4. Albarello M.	ITA	1:23:55.7
5. Jevne E.	NOR	1:24:07.7
6. Majback C.	SWE	1:24:12.1
7. Jonsson N.	SWE	1:25:17.6
8. Ponsiluoma J.	SWE	1:25:24.4
9. Smirnov W.	EUN	1:25:27.6
10. Kirvesniemi H.	FIN	1:25:28.5

CROSS COUNTRY SKIING MEN, 10km CLASSICAL - PURSUIT

1. ULVANG V.	NOR	27:36.0
2. ALBARELLO M.	ITA	27:55.2
3. MAJBACK C.	SWE	27:56.4
4. DAEHLIE B.	NOR	28:01.6
5. JONSSON N.	SWE	28:03.1
6. KIRVESNIEMI H.	FIN	28:23.3
7. VANZETTA G.	ITA	28:26.9
8. STADLOBER A.	AUT	28:27.5
9. MOGREN T.	SWE	28:37.8
10. FAUNER S.	ITA	28:53.8

CROSS COUNTRY SKIING MEN, 15 kmFREE - PURSUIT

1. DAEHLIE B.	NOR	1:05:37.9	
2. ULVANG V.	NOR	1:06:31.3	
3. VANZETTA G.	ITA	1:06:32.2	
4. ALBARELLO M.	ITA	1:06:33.3	
5. MOGREN T.	SWE	1:06:37.4	
6. MAJBACK C.	SWE	1:07:17.0	
7. FAUNER S.	ITA	1:07:34.9	
8. SMIRNOV W.	EUN	1:07:35.8	
9. FORSBERG H.	SWE	1:07:52.4	
10. STADLOBER A.	AUT	1:07:57.6	

CROSS COUNTRY SKIING MEN, RELAY 4x10km MIX

1. LANGLI T.	NOR	1:39:26.0
ULVANG V.		
SKJELDAL K.		
DAEHLIE B.		
2. PULIE G.	ITA	1:40:52.7
ALBARELLO M.		
VANZETTA G.		
FAUNER S.		
3. KUUSISTO M.	FIN	1:41:22.9
KIRVESNIEMI H.		
RASANEN J.		
ISOMETSA J.		
4. OTTOSSON J.	SWE	1:41:23.1
MAJBACK C.		
FORSBERG H.		
MOGREN T.		
5. KIRILLOV A.	EUN	1:43:03.6
SMIRNOV W.		
BOTVINOV M.		
PROKUROROV A.		
6. BAUROTH H.	GER	1:43:41.7
BEHLE J.		
REIN T.		
MUHLEGG J.		
7. NYC R.	TCH	1:44:20.0
BUCHTA L.		
BENC P.		
KORUNKA V.		
8. REMY P.	FRA	1:44:51.1
SANCHEZ P.		
AZAMBRE S.		
BALLAND H.		
9. SCHWARZ A.	AUT	1:45:56.6
STADLOBER A.		
MARENT A.		
RINGHOFER A.		
10. VEERPALU A.	EST	1:46:33.3
TEPPAN J.		
KASSIN E.		
VALBE U.		

CROSS-COUNTRY SKIING MEN, 50km FREE TECHNIQUE

1. DAEHLIE B.	NOR	2:03:41.5
2. DE ZOLT M.	ITA	2:04:39.1
3. VANZETTA G.	ITA	2:06:42.1
4. PROKUROROV A.	EUN	2:07:06.1
5. BALLAND H.	FRA	2:07:17.7
6. NYC R.	TCH	2:07:41.5
7. MUHLEGG J.	GER	2:07:45.2
8. BENC P.	TCH	2:08:13.6
9. ULVANG V.	NOR	2:08:21.5
10. POLVARA G.	ITA	2:09:27.8

NORDIC COMBINED, INDIVIDUAL

1. GUY F.	FRA	0.0 behind
2. GUILLAUME S.	FRA	48.4 behind
3. SULZENBACHER K.	AUT	1:06.3 behind
4. LUNDBERG F.	NOR	1:26.7 behind
5. OFNER K.	AUT	1:29.8 behind
6. LEVANDI A.	EST	1:34.1 behind
7. OGIWARA K.	JPN	1:57.4 behind
8. USTUPSKI S.	POL	2:28.1 behind
9. ELDEN T.	NOR	2:43.8 behind
10. APELAND K.	NOR	..2:55.8 behind

NORDIC COMBINED, TEAM

1. MIKATA R.	JPN	0.0 behind
KONO T.		
OGIWARA K.		
2. APELAND K.	NOR	1:26.4 behind
LUNDBERG F.		
ELDEN T.		
3. OFNER K.	AUT	1:40.1 behind
KREINER S.		
SULZENBACHER K.		
4. REPELLIN F.	FRA	2:15.5 behind
GUILLAUME S.		
GUY F		
5. POHL H.P.	GER	4:45.4 behind
DEIMEL J.		
DUFTER T.		
6. KOVARIK J.	TCH	9:04.7 behind
KUCERA M.		
MAKA F.		
7. SAAPUNKI P.	FIN	9:06.8 behind
MANTILA J.		
SUMMANEN T.		
8. HOLLAND J.	USA	9:08.3 behind
TETREAULT T.		
HECKMAN R.		
9. MARKVARDT A.	EST	9:40.4 behind
HELI P.		
LEVANDI A.		
10. KEMPF H.	SUI	10:01.9 behind
SCHAAD		
ZARUCCHI M.		

SKI JUMPING, K90m

1. VETTORI E.	AUT	222.8 points
2. HOLLWARTH M.	AUT	218.1 points
3. NIEMINEN T.	FIN	217.0 points
4. Kuttin H.	AUT	214.4 points
5. Laitinen M.	FIN	213.6 points
6. Felder A.	AUT	213.5 points
7. Hunger H.	GER	211.6 points
8. Mollard D.	FRA	209.7 points
9. Weissflog J.	GER	208.5 points
10. Parma J.	TCH	207.9 points

SKI JUMPING, K120m TEAM

1. NIKKOLA A.P.	FIN	644.4
LAITINEN M.		
LAAKKONEN R.		
NIEMINEN T.		
2. KUTTIN H.	AUT	642.9
VETTORI E.		
HOLLWARTH M.		
FELDER A.		
3. GODER T.	TCH	620.1
JEZ F.		
SAKALA J.		
PARMA J.		
4. KAMIHARAKO J.	JPN	571.0
HARADA M.		
KASAI N.		
SUDA K.		
5. HUNGER H.	GER	544.6
THOMA D.		
DUFFNER C.		
WEISSFLOG J.		
6. KOPAC P.	SLO	543.3
ZUPAN M.		
PETEK F.		
GOSTISA S.		
7. OLIJNYK R.	NOR	538.0
JOHANSEN M.		
OTTESEN L.		
BREDESEN E.		
8. GAHLER M.	SUI	537.9
TRUNZ M.		
FREIHOLZ S.		
ZUEND S.		
9. WESTMAN M.	SWE	515.1
BOKLOV J.		
TALLBERG S.		
MARTINSSON M.		
10. DELAUP S.	FRA	510.9
JEAN-PROST N.		
MOLLARD D.		
GAY J.		

SKI JUMPING, K120m

1. NIEMINEN T.	FIN	239.5
2. HOLLWARTH M.	AUT	227.3
3. KUTTIN H.	AUT	214.8
4. HARADA M.	JPN	211.3
5. PARMA J.	TCH	198.0
6. DELAUP S.	FRA	185.6
7. LUNARDI I.	ITA	185.2
8. PETEK F.	SLO	177.1
9. FELDER A.	AUT	176.9
10. ESSINE M.	EUN	176.5

BIATHLON LADIES, 7.5km SPRINT

1. RESTZOVA A.	EUN	24:29.2
2. MISERSKY A.	GER	24:45.1
3. BELOVA E.	EUN	24:50.8
4. ALEXIEVA N.	BUL	24:55.8
5. ADAMICKOVA J.	TCH	24:57.6
6. SCHAAF P.	GER	25:10.4
7. BRIAND A.	FRA	25:29.8
8. BLAGOEVA S.	BUL	25:33.5
9. BURLET D.	FRA	25:50.5
10. KESPER I.	GER	25:57.3

BIATHLON LADIES, RELAY 3x7.5km

1. NIOGRET C.	FRA	1:15:55.6
CLAUDEL V.		
BRIAND A.		
2. GER DISL U.	GER	1:16:18.4
MISERSKY A.		
SCHAAF P.		
3. BELOVA E.	EUN	1:16:54.6
RESTZOVA A.		
MELNIKOVA E.		
4. BLAGOEVA S.	BUL	1:18:54.8
ALEXIEVA N.		
SCHKODREVA I.		
5. LAMPINEN M.	FIN	1:20:17.8
SIKIO T.		
MARKKANEN T.		
6. EKLUND C.	SWE	1:20:56.6
BJORKBOM I.		
STADIG M.		
7. TROSTEN S.	NOR	1:21:20.0
FOSSEN H.		
KRISTIANSEN E.		
8. SUVOVA G.	TCH	1:23:12.7
KULHAVA J.		
ADAMICKOVA J.		
9. POLJAKOVA J.	EST	1:23:16.2
PETERSON E.		
LEPIK K.		
10. SOTROPA A.	ROM	1:23:39.6
CARSTOI M.		
ANOSIU H.		

BIATHLON LADIES, 15km

1. MYSERSKY A.	GER	51:47.2
2. PECHERSKAIA S.	EUN	51:58.5
3. BEDARD M.	CAN	52:15.0
4. CLAUDEL V.	FRA	52:21.2
5. ALEXIEVA N.	BUL	52:30.2
6. BURLET D.	FRA	53:00.8
7. NIOGRET C.	FRA	53:06.6
8. SANTER N.	ITA	53:10.3
9. KRISTIANSEN E.	NOR	53:19.6
10. TROSTEN S.	NOR	53:24.5

BIATHLON MEN, 10km SPRINT

1. KIRCHNER M.	GER	26:02.3
2. GROSS R.	GER	26:18.0
3. ELORANTA H.	FIN	26:26.6
4. TCHEPIKOV S.	EUN	26:27.5
5. KIRIENKO V.	EUN	26:31.8
6. STEINIGEN J.	GER	26:34.8
7. ZINGERLE A.	ITA	26:38.6
8. CYR S.	CAN	26:46.4
9. ROTSCH F.P.	GER	26:54.1
10. FLANDIN H.	FRA	26:56.6

BIATHLON MEN, RELAY 4x7.5km

1. GROSS R.	GER	1:24:43.5
STEINIGEN J.		
KIRCHNER M.		
FISCHER F.		
2. MEDVEDEV V.	EUN	1:25:06.3
POPOV A.		
KIRIENKO V.		
TCHEPIKOV S.		
3. JOHANSSON U.	SWE	1:25:38.2
ANDERSSON L.		
WIKSTEN T.		
LOFGREN M.		
4. LEITGEB H.	ITA	1:26:18.1
PASSLER J.		
CARRARA P.		
ZINGERLE A.		
5. EINANG G.	NOR	1:26:32.4
LOBERG F.		
FENNE G.		
KVALFOSS E.		
6. BLOND X.	FRA	1:27:13.3
GERBIER T.		
DUMONT C.		
FLANDIN H.		
7. RYPL M.	TCH	1:27:15.7
KOS T.		
HOLUBEC J.		
MASARIK I.		
8. HIETALAHTI V.	FIN	1:27:39.5
NIEMI J.		
ELORANTA H.		
KATAJA K.		
9. KOZLOWSKI D.	POL	1:27:56.7
ZIEMIANIN J.		
WOJTAS J.		
SOSNA K.		
10. RUPERTUS G.	CAN	1:29:37.3
PAQUET J.		
FIALA T.		
CYR S.		

BIATHLON MEN, 20km

1.	REDKINE E.	EUN	57:34.4
2.	KIRCHNER M.	GER	57:40.8
3.	LOFGREN M.	SWE	57:59.4
4.	POPOV A.	EUN	58:02.9
5.	ELORANTA H.	FIN	58:15.7
6.	HIETALAHTI V.	FIN	58:24.6
7.	PASSLER J.	ITA	58:25.9
8.	LOBERG F.	NOR	58:32.4
9.	FENNE G.	NOR	58:47.6
10.	TCHEPIKOV S.	EUN	59:12.6

FINAL STANDING

1.	UNIFIED TEAM
2.	CANADA
3.	CZECHOSLOVAKIA
4.	USA
5.	SWEDEN
6.	GERMANY
7.	FINLAND
8.	FRANCE
9.	NORWAY
10.	SWITZERLAND

ICE HOCKEY
FINALES PLAY OFF

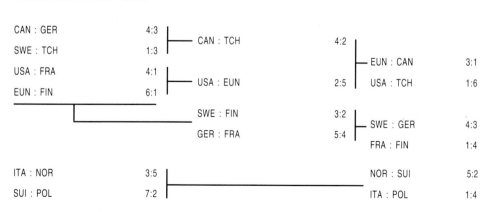

CAN : GER	4:3	
SWE : TCH	1:3	CAN : TCH 4:2
USA : FRA	4:1	
EUN : FIN	6:1	USA : EUN 2:5
		EUN : CAN 3:1
		USA : TCH 1:6
SWE : FIN	3:2	
GER : FRA	5:4	SWE : GER 4:3
		FRA : FIN 1:4
ITA : NOR	3:5	
SUI : POL	7:2	NOR : SUI 5:2
		ITA : POL 1:4

BOBSLED, TWO

1.	WEDER G.	SUI-1	04:03.26
	ACKLIN D.		
2.	LOCHNER R.	GER-1	04:03.55
	ZIMMERMANN M.		
3.	LANGEN C.	GER-2	04:03.63
	EGER G.		
4.	APPELT I.	AUT-2	04:03.67
	SCHROLL T.		
5.	HUBER G.	ITA-1	04:03.72
	TICCI S.		
6.	TOUT M.	GBR-1	04:03.87
	PAUL L.		
7.	SHIMER B.	USA-1	04:03.95
	WALKER H.		
8.	RAINER G.	AUT-1	04:04.00
	BACHLER T.		
9.	MARINEAU D.	CAN-2	04:04.08
	FARSTAD C.		
10.	MEILI C.	SUI-2	04:04.36
	REICH C.		

BOBSLED, FOUR

1.	APPELT I.	AUT-1	3:53.90
	WINKLER H.		
	HAIDACHER G.		
	SCHROLL T.		
2.	HOPPE W.	GER-1	3:53.92
	MUSIOL B.		
	KUHN A.		
	HANNEMANN R.		
3.	WEDER G.	SUI-1	3:54.13
	ACKLIN D.		
	SCHINDELHOLZ L.		
	MORELL C.		
4.	LORI C.	CAN-1	3:54.24
	LEBLANC K.P.L.		
	LANGFORD C.		
	MAC EACHERN D.		
5.	MEILI C.	SUI-2	3:54.38
	GERBER B.		
	REICH C.		
	LOFFLER G.		
6.	CZUDAJ H.	GER-2	3:54.42
	BONK T.		
	JANG A.		
	SZELIG A.		
7.	TOUT M.	GBR-1	3:54.89
	FARREL G.		
	FIELD P.		
	PAUL L.		
8.	FLACHER C.	FRA-1	3:54.91
	DASSE C.		
	TRIBONDEAU T.		
	FOURMIGUE G.		
9.	WILL R.	USA-1	3:54.92
	SAWYER J.		
	KIRBY K.		
	COLEMAN C.T.		
10.	RAINER G.	AUT-2	3:55.01
	BACHLER T.		
	NENTWIG C.		
	SCHUTZENAUER M.		

LUGE MEN, SINGLES

1.	HACKL G.	GER	3:02.363
2.	PROCK M.	AUT	3:02.669
3.	SCHMIDT M.	AUT	3:02.942
4.	Huber N.	ITA	3:02.973
5.	Muller J.	GER	3:03.197
6.	Manzenreiter R.	AUT	3:03.267
7.	Haselrieder O.	ITA	3:03.276
8.	Friedl R.	GER	3:03.543
9.	Danilin S.	EUN	3:03.773
10.	Kennedy D.	USA	3:03.852

LUGE LADIES, SINGLES

1.	NEUNER D.	AUT	3:06.696
2.	NEUNER A.	AUT	3:06.769
3.	ERDMANN S.	GER	3:07.115
4.	WEISSENSTEINER G.	ITA	3:07.673
5.	MYLER C.	USA	3:07.973
6.	KOHLISCH G.	GER	3:07.980
7.	TAGWERKER A.	AUT	3:08.018
8.	JAKOUCHENKO N.	EUN	3:08.383
9.	TERWILLEGAR E.	USA	3:08.547
10.	GUBKINA I.	EUN	3:08.746

LUGE MEN, DOUBLES

1.	KRAUSSE S.	GER	1:32.053
	BEHRENDT J.		
2.	MANKEL Y.	GER	1:32.239
	RUDOLPH T.		
3.	RAFFL H.	ITA	1:32.298
	HUBER N.		
4.	APOSTOL I.	ROM	1:32.649
	CEPI L.		
5.	BRUGGER K.	ITA	1:32.810
	HUBER W.		
6.	KOHALA H.	SWE	1:33.134
	LINDQUIST C.J.		
7.	GLEIRSCHER G.	AUT	1:33.257
	SCHMIDT M.		
8.	DEMTSCHENKO A.	EUN	1:33.299
	SELENSKI A.		
9.	SUCKOW W.	USA	1:33.451
	TAVARES B.		
10.	LOBANOV I.	EUN	1:33.947
	BELAJKOV G.		

FIGURE SKATING MEN

1.	PETRENKO V.	EUN	1.0 points
2.	WYLIE P.	USA	2.0 points
3.	BARNA P.	TCH	3.0 points
4.	BOWMAN C.	USA	4.0 points
5.	OURMANOV A.	EUN	5.0 points
6.	BROWNING K.	CAN	6.0 points
7.	STOJKO E.	CAN	7.0 points
8.	ZAGORODNIUK V.	EUN	8.0 points
9.	SLIPCHUK M.	CAN	9.0 points
10.	FILIPOWSKI G.	POL	10.0 points

FIGURE SKATING, PAIRS

1.	MICHKOUTENIOK N.		
	DMITRIEV A.	EUN	1.5 points
2.	BETCHKE E.		
	PETROV D.	EUN	3.0 points
3.	BRASSEUR I.		
	EISLER L.	CAN	4.5 points
4.	KOVARIKOVA R.		
	NOVOTNY R.	TCH	6.0 points
5.	CHICHKOVA E.		
	NAOUMOV V.	EUN	7.5 points
6.	KUCHIKI N.		
	SAND T.	USA	9.0 points
7.	SCHWARZ P.		
	KONIG A.	GER	11.0 points
8.	WOTZEL M.		
	RAUSCHENBACH A.	GER	13.0 points
9.	HOUGH C.		
	LADRET D.	CAN	14.5 points
10.	URBANSKI C.		
	MARVAL R.	USA	14.5 points

FIGURE SKATING LADIES, ICE DANCING

1.	KLIMOVA M.		
	PONOMARENKO S.	EUN	2.0 points
2.	DUCHESNAY-DEAN I.		
	DUCHESNAY P.	FRA	4.4 points
3.	USOVA M.		
	ZHULIN A.	EUN	5.6 points
4.	GRITSCHUK O.		
	PLATOV E.	EUN	8.0 points
5.	CALEGARI S.		
	CAMERLENGO P.	ITA	10.0 points
6.	RAHKAMO S.		
	KOKKO P.	FIN	12.4 points
7.	ENGI K.		
	TOTH A.	HUN	13.6 points
8.	YVON D.		
	PALLUEL F.	FRA	16.6 points
9.	MONIOTTE S.		
	LAVANCHY P.	FRA	17.4 points
10.	MRAZOVA K.		
	SIMECEK M.	TCH	20.6 points

FIGURE SKATING LADIES

1.	YAMAGUCHI K.	USA	1.5 points
2.	ITO M.	JPN	4.0 points
3.	KERRIGAN N.	USA	4.0 points
4.	HARDING T.	USA	7.0 points
5.	BONALY S.	FRA	7.5 points
6.	CHEN L.	CHN	10.5 points
7.	SATO Y.	JPN	10.5 points
8.	PRESTON K.	CAN	14.0 points
9.	CHOUINARD J.	CAN	16.0 points
10.	KIELMANN M.	GER	16.5 points

SPEED SKATING LADIES, 3000m

1.	NIEMANN G.	GER	04:19,90
2.	WARNICKE H.	GER	04:22.88
3.	HUNYADY E.	AUT	04:24.64
4.	Zijlstra C.	NED	04:27.18
5.	Boiko S.	EUN	04:28.00
6.	Van Gennip Y.	NED	04:28.10
7.	Bajanova S.	EUN	04:28.19
8.	Boerner J.	GER	04:28.52
9.	Van Schie L.	NED	04:30.57
10.	Prokacheva L.	EUN	04:30.76

SPEED SKATING LADIES, 500m

1.	BLAIR B.	USA	00:40.33
2.	YE Q.	CHN	00:40.51
3.	LUDING C.	GER	00:40.57
4.	Garbrecht M.	GER	00:40.63
5.	Aaftink C.	NED	00:40.66
6.	Auch S.	CAN	00:40.83
7.	Shimazaki K.	JPN	00:40.98
8.	Hauck A.	GER	00:41.10
9.	You S.H.	KOR	00:41.28
10.	Baier A.	GER	00:41.30

SPEED SKATING LADIES, 1500m

1.	BOERNER J.	GER	02:05.87
2.	NIEMANN G.	GER	02:05.92
3.	HASHIMOTO S.	JPN	02:06.88
4.	POLOZKOVA N.	EUN	02:07.12
5.	GARBRECHT M.	GER	02:07.24
6.	BAJANOVA S.	EUN	02:07.81
7.	HUNYADY E.	AUT	02:08.29
8.	WARNICKE H.	GER	02:08.52
9.	ZIJLSTRA C.	NED	02:08.54
10.	PROKACHEVA L.	EUN	02:08.71

SPEED SKATING LADIES, 1000m

1.	BLAIR B.	USA	01:21.90
2.	YE Q.	CHN	01:21.92
3.	GARBRECHT M.	GER	01:22.10
4.	AAFTINK C.	NED	01:22.60
5.	HASHIMOTO S.	JPN	01:22.63
6.	DASCALU M.	ROM	01:22.85
7.	TIOUCHNIAKOVA E.	EUN	01:22.97
8.	LUDING C.	GER	01:23.06
9.	BAIER A.	GER	01:23.31
10.	HUNYADY E.	AUT	01:23.40

BRINGING YOU BETTER LIGHT
Because light is life

Philips Lighting

PHILIPS

SPEED SKATING LADIES, 5000m

1.	NIEMANN G.	GER	07:31.57
2.	WARNICKE H.	GER	07:37.59
3.	PECHSTEIN C.	GER	07:39.80
4.	ZIJLSTRA C.	NED	07:41.10
5.	PROKACHEVA L.	EUN	07:41.65
6.	BOIKO S.	EUN	07:44.19
7.	BAJANOVA S.	EUN	07:45.55
8.	VAN SCHIE L.	NED	07:46.94
9.	HASHIMOTO S.	JPN	07:47.65
10.	BELCI DAL FARRA	ITA	07:50.42

SPEED SKATING MEN, 5000m

1.	KARLSTAD G.	NOR	06:59.97
2.	ZANDSTRA F.	NED	07:02.28
3.	VISSER L.	NED	07:04.96
4.	DITTRICH F.	GER	07:06.33
5.	VELDKAMP B.	NED	07:08.00
6.	FLAIM E.	USA	07:11.15
7.	KOSS J.	NOR	07:11.32
8.	SANAROV E.	EUN	07:11.38
9.	SCHON J.	SWE	07:12.15
10.	HADSCHIEFF M.	AUT	07:12.97

SPEED SKATING MEN, 500m

1.	MEY U.J.	GER	00:37.14
2.	KUROIWA T.	JPN	00:37.18
3.	INOUE J.	JPN	00:37.26
4.	JANSEN D.	USA	00:37.46
5.	VAN VELDE G.	NED	00:37.49
5.	MIYABE Y.	JPN	00:37.49
7.	GOLOUBEV A.	EUN	00:37.51
8.	JELEZOVSKI I.	EUN	00:37.57
9.	SONG C.	CHN	00:37.58
10.	KIM Y.M.	KOR	00:37.60

SPEED SKATING MEN, 1500m

1.	KOSS J.	NOR	01:54.81
2.	SONDRAL A.	NOR	01:54.85
3.	VISSER L.	NED	01:54.90
4.	RITSMA R.	NED	01:55.70
5.	VELDKAMP B.	NED	01:56.33
6.	ZINKE O.	GER	01:56.74
7.	ZANDSTRA F.	NED	01:56.96
8.	KARLSTAD G.	NOR	01:56.98
9.	MIYABE Y.	JPN	01:56.99
10.	JELEZOVSKI I.	EUN	01:57.24

SPEED SKATING MEN, 1000m

1.	ZINKE O.	GER	01:14.85
2.	KIM Y.M.	KO	01:14.86
3.	MIYABE Y.	JPN	01:14.92
4.	VAN VELDE G.	NED	01:14.93
5.	ADEBERG P.	GER	01:15.04
6.	JELEZOVSKI I.	EUN	01:15.05
7.	THIBAULT G.	CAN	01:15.36
8.	GOULIAEV N.	EUN	01:15.46
9.	KUROIWA T.	JPN	01:15.56
10.	ZANDSTRA F.	NED	01:15.57

SPEED SKATING MEN, 10000m

1.	VELDKAMP B.	NED	14:12.12
2.	KOSS J.	NOR	14:14.58
3.	KARLSTAD G.	NOR	14:18.13
4.	VUNDERINK R.	NED	14:22.92
5.	SATO K.	JPN	14:28.30
6.	HADSCHIEFF M.	AUT	14:28.80
7.	BENGTSSON P.	SWE	14:35.58
8.	JOHANSEN S.	NOR	14:36.09
9.	SIGHEL R.	ITA	14:38.23
10.	SANAROV E.	EUN	14:38.99

SHORT TRACK SPEED SKATING LADIES 3000m RELAY

1. CANADA	
2. UNITED STATES	
3. UNIFIED TEAM	
4. JAPAN	
5. FRANCE	
6. NEDERLANDS	
7. ITALY	

SHORT TRACK SPEED SKATING LADIES, 500m

1.	TURNER C.		USA
2.	LI Y.		CHN
3.	HWANG O.S.		PRK
4.	VELZEBOER M.		NED
5.	PYLAEVA M.		EUN
6.	LAMBERT N.		CAN
7.	VLASOVA I.		EUN
8.	WANG X.		CHN
9.	KIM S.H.		KOR
10.	YAMADA N.		JAP

SHORT TRACK SPEED SKATING MEN, 1000m

1.	KIM K.H.		KOR
2.	BLACKBURN F.		CAN
3.	LEE J.H.		KOR
4.	MCMILLEN M.		NZL
5.	O'REILLY W.		GBR
6.	BLANCHART G.		BEL
7.	LACKIE M.		CAN
8.	DAIGNAULT M.		CAN
9.	JASPER M.		GBR
10.	VELZEBOER M.		NED

SHORT TRACK SPEED SKATING MEN 5000m RELAY

1.	KOREA	KOR
2.	CANADA	CAN
3.	JAPAN	JPN
4.	NEW ZEALAND	NZL
5.	FRANCE	FRA
6.	GREAT BRITAIN	GBR
7.	AUSTRALIA	AUS
8.	ITALY	ITA
9.	BELGIUM	BEL

MEDALS

POSITION	NATION	GOLD	SILVER	BRONZE	TOTAL
1	GER	10	10	6	26
2	EUN	9	6	8	23
3	NOR	9	6	5	20
4	AUT	6	7	8	21
5	USA	5	4	2	11
6	ITA	4	6	4	14
7	FRA	3	5	1	9
8	FIN	3	1	3	7
9	CAN	2	3	2	7
10	KOR	2	1	1	4
11	JPN	1	2	4	7
12	NED	1	1	2	4
13	SWE	1	0	3	4
14	SUI	1	0	2	3
15	CHN	0	3	0	3
16	LUX	0	2	0	2
17	NZL	0	1	0	1
18	TCH	0	0	3	3
19	ESP	0	0	1	1
19	PRK	0	0	1	1

Thanks for the hand

Almost a hundred years ago the founder of the Modern Olympic Movement, Baron Pierre de Coubertin gave a speech in which he said "The important thing in the Olympic Games is not to win but to take part."

This February the eyes of the world are turned towards Albertville to witness more than 60 nations taking part in the 1992 Winter Olympic Games.

It is the generous support, the helping hand of our sponsors, given in so many ways, which enables the world's finest athletes to participate in these Games and unite in a common pursuit of excellence.

On behalf of the Olympic Movement we thank you the Worldwide Olympic Sponsors for your generosity,

your technology, your ingenuity, your enthusiasm and above all your belief in the Spirit of the Games and the importance of universal friendship.

In that same historic speech, de Coubertin spoke of the nobility of struggle, not merely of triumph. "Not to have conquered, but to have fought well." His closing words were "To spread these precepts is to build up a more valiant, more strong and above all, more scrupulous and more generous humanity."

The valued contribution of all the sponsors to the 1992 Games has proven their generosity and gift to humanity. We appreciate this opportunity to demonstrate our gratitude.

The Worldwide Olympic Sponsors – 1992

Created and produced by **GREY/GCI** Communications Agency to the International Olympic Committee

THE PHENOMENON
OF OLYMPIC PIN TRADING

F rom its early beginning in Europe tot the 1984 Summer
Games in Los Angeles and more recently the 1988 Winter Games in Calgary, Olympic pin collecting is hotter than ever.
And nowhere does the passion for the pins run as deep it does in France, where the nationwide frenzy over the
tiny badges even has it own name, «pinsomania».

This craze, however, is no passing fad. Once the Olympic torch for the Albertville Games is extinguished, pin collectors,
Olympic organizations and sponsors will begin looking to Summer Games in Barcelona, and then beyond to the
1994 Winter Games in Lillehamer, Norway.

Le Comité d'organisation des XVIes Jeux olympiques d'hiver d'Albertville et de la Savoie et le Comité International Olympique remercient les entreprises partenaires pour leur soutien indispensable à l'organisation des Jeux.
Elles ont su mobiliser ce qu'elles avaient de meilleur, leur richesse humaine, leur compétence et leur expérience au service de l'idéal olympique.

The Organizing Committee of the XVI Olympic Winter Games of Albertville and Savoie and the International Olympic Committee thank their partners for their unfailing support so vital to the organization of the Games.
They have dedicated the best of their human resources and unparalleled expertise in their respective fields to the benefit of the Olympic ideal.

AGF ▪ SNCF ▪ EVIAN
ALCATEL ▪ RENAULT
▪ CANDIA-YOPLAIT ▪
▪ CRÉDIT LYONNAIS ▪
▪ IBM ▪ FRANCE TELECOM ▪
▪ BIS ▪ LA POSTE ▪ THOMSON ▪

WORLDWIDE SPONSORS
1992 OLYMPIC GAMES

COCA-COLA ▪ KODAK ▪
PHILIPS ▪ BROTHER ▪ 3M
▪ MARS ▪ PANASONIC
BAUSCH & LOMB ▪ VISA
▪ TIME-SPORTS ILLUSTRATED ▪
▪ RICOH ▪ U.S. POSTAL SERVICE ▪

I M P R E S S U M

OFFICIAL BOOK OF THE XVI OLYMPIC
WINTER GAMES
ALBERTVILLE '92

Published by
IMS/STUDIO 6 - LAUSANNE

This Book is fully licensed and approved by
the International Olympic Committee and by
the Organizing Committee of the XVI
Olympic Winter Games Albertville '92.

IMS/STUDIO 6 thanks the following people
for their invaluable help in the preparation of
this Book, without whom its publication
would not have been possible in such space
of time.

Director:
Goran A. TAKATCH
Art Director:
Muris CAMO
Design:
Eric JACQUARD
Sabrina TARCHINI
Photography Director:
Carla TRACCANELLA SCHNEPP
Photography Editor:
Maarten VAN DER ENDE
Production Coordination:
Olivier COULET
Marketing:
Christophe STADLER
Texts:
H.E. Juan Antonio SAMARANCH,
IOC President
COJO ALBERTVILLE '92
David MILLER
Special USA section:
Stephen WOODWARD
Statistics:
Namik DZUMISIC

Photography:
THE ALLSPORT PHOTOGRAPHIC
TEAM:
Director of Photography:
Steve POWELL

Bob MARTIN
Simon BRUTY
Mike POWELL
Pascal RONDEAU
Chris COLE
Shaun BOTTERILL
Rick STEWART
Nathan BILOW
Henry DOBKIN
Lee FARRANT
Gary PRIOR

THE VANDYSTADT/ALLSPORT
FRANCE TEAM
Chief Photographer and Director:
Gerard VANDYSTADT

Yann GUICHAOUA
Richard MARTIN
Bernard ASSET
Gerard PLANCHENAULT
Eric PAGE
Francis BOMPARD
Jean-Louis FEL
Alain GROSCLAUDE
Michel COTTIN
Benoit BUFFET
Roland THIEVENNAZ

ALAIN ERNOULT FEATURES:
Dingo
Alain ERNOULT

COJO:
Françoise. SKOTNICKA

IMS/STUDIO 6:
Carla TRACCANELLA
Maarten VAN DER ENDE

Special thanks to:

ALPES MICRO EDITION
Laurent BAGNIS COJO
Anne-Lise BORBOEN WAECHTER
Catherine CHAUMELY COJO
Denis ECHARD IOC
Raymond GAFNER IOC
Garage JAN - Lausanne
Lee MARTIN ALLSPORT
Benoit ROCHER
Marie-Hélène ROUKHADZE
Matti SALMENKILA IOC PRESS
COMMISSION
Roland SCHNEPP
Vera TAKATCH
Michèle VERDIER IOC
Mr & Ms SCHWINTE & family thanks to
whom our stay in Albertville was made
possible.

Colour separations, printing and binding:
ROYAL SMEETS OFFSET, Weert

Published under authority of the
International Olympic Committee and the
Organizing Committee of the XVI Olympic
Winter Games Albertville '92 (COJO).

Grammar and spelling checks by software
«GRAMMATIK».

All the photographs in this Book were
taken exclusively on KODAK films and
processed in KODAK laboratories in the
Main Press Centre Albertville '92.

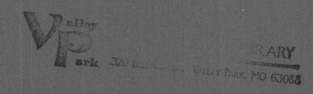